Light and Legacies

Light and Legacies

Stories of Black Girlhood and Liberation

Janaka Bowman Lewis

THE UNIVERSITY OF
SOUTH CAROLINA PRESS

© 2023 University of South Carolina

Published by the University of South Carolina Press
Columbia, South Carolina 29208

www.uscpress.com

Manufactured in the United States of America

32 31 30 29 28 27 26 25 24 23
10 9 8 7 6 5 4 3 2 1

Library of Congress Cataloging-in-Publication Data
can be found at http://catalog.loc.gov/.

ISBN 978-1-64336-385-1 (hardcover)
ISBN 978-1-64336-386-8 (paperback)
ISBN 978-1-64336-387-5 (ebook)

Excerpts of Chapters 4 and 5 are found in the following:
Lewis, Janaka Bowman. "Building the Worlds of Our Dreams: Black Girlhood and Quare
    Narratives in African American Literature." *South (Chapel Hill, NC)* 51, no. 1 (2018): 96–114.
    ———. "Handle Us Warmly: Girlhood, Community and Radical Creativity in *for colored
    girls.*" *CLA Journal* 62, no. 2 (2019): 202–12.

The work in this book has spanned a lifetime, as I have told stories (mine and others') since my own girlhood. I dedicate it to those who were girls with me and to those who kept us and our spirit of girlhood alive.

And to my family, especially the little lights.

Photo by author

In Memoriam, SDR (Feb. 1981–Oct. 2021)

"*We was girls once*"
and we played, like really, truly played.
Softball, basketball, and as the boys remember, "get like me."
You were loud as hell, and nobody better piss you off.
Your mouth outtalked your game.
I always thought that the smallest ones (in height, although
  large in presence) needed to be heard the most.—j. b. lewis

ﻮ:ﻮ

Contents

Prologue

The Gift

Where it all began.

In first grade (in the mid-1980s, in my childhood hometown of Augusta, Georgia), I won a poetry contest where every poem each student memorized earned a dot on a bright red paper ladybug with our names. The person with the most dots at the end was the winner and got a poetry book, a whole book just for them. I had started memorizing Shel Silverstein poems with my best friend from kindergarten already—we would recite them during afternoon conversations on our parents' landline phones—so I was ahead to start, and I won by one dot after a close finish (I think; at least it makes for a better story). My teacher Mrs. Parker, a gray-haired, then-seemingly "much older" white woman from Lexington, Kentucky, gave me Nikki Giovanni's *Spin a Soft Black Song* as the prize. I still don't know whether she picked it out before I won or had an option of books to choose from (as any teacher should) or whether she just decided that whoever won should have that book, but whatever the case, it was a gift.

As a middle child (of three girls and, later, a baby brother), I didn't have a lot of things that were just mine. I did have my own room, located between my sisters' and my parents' rooms, with a twin bed and colorful boxes on three walls and the remaining painted bright yellow like sunshine. I remember trips to the store to choose wallpaper, though I do not remember if those boxes were already on the wall when we moved in. I could look through the windows at the yard outside, and there was more yard out back. I went to school in the middle, behind my sister who was one grade ahead and ahead of the baby girl, not always the youngest but called the baby girl for most of her life because she wouldn't leave my mother's side.

I had many of my own possessions then, and for a child born in the 1980s, it was also a gift to always have dolls, toys, and book characters that looked like me. Books belonged to the family (although I had my own built-in desk with shelves). *Spin a Soft Black Song*, however, was my book, my gift, which let me know not only that I mattered (which I already knew—my family let me know that I was born for whatever success I determined) but that others knew that Black children mattered, too.

In the prologue, Giovanni wrote, "I seek the courage of a boy . . . who could go into the Temple to assail the knowledge of the Elders . . . The confidence of a man . . . to pronounce the earth a satellite of the sun . . . The curiosity of a woman . . . to see not only those aspects unseen but those unseeable. I share the desire to plant a masthead for doves . . . to spin a soft Black song . . . to waltz with the children . . . to the mountains of our dreams" (p. vi). As I attend as many of Giovanni's live talks as I can, I have heard her say similar things about what men are able to do, even as she wrote her famous poem "Ego Tripping (there must be a reason why)" as a response. Here, however, she offers that the curiosity of women enable her—enable *us*—to see "not only those aspects unseen but those unseeable." We have to see each other as Black women and in community, in all our complexities, in order to see our children *and* to dance together, and the soft Black song, not the hardness dictated upon us and our lives, is the goal we want to achieve.

I write this book as a remembrance for the lives of Black girlhood lived and living but also as a requiem for the lives of the little Black girls lost, in Birmingham in 1963, where my telling of Black girlhood stories began in a summer seminar that followed my eighth-grade year, but also before and throughout my entire life. I also write of the activism that has created spaces for Black girls to move, to breathe, to live, from Harriet Jacobs and Elizabeth Keckley in the 1860s to Charlotte Hawkins Brown in 1940, to Angela Davis in the 1960s and 1970s, to Toni Morrison and, recently, to Angie Thomas through fiction and Monique Morris's agency through telling the real, lived stories of Black girls whom society deems "unmanageable" but in whom she finds the tremendous joy that we know exists.

Nazera Sadiq Wright's *Black Girlhood in the Nineteenth Century* (2016) provides an excellent framework for texts published before 1900 that represent Black girls. *Light and Legacies* is also part of a larger dialogue amongst social and performative texts about Black girlhood, including Kyra Gaunt's *The Games Black Girls Play: Learning the Ropes from Double-Dutch to Hip-Hop* (2006); Ruth Nicole Brown's *Black Girlhood Celebration: Toward a Hip-Hop Feminist Pedagogy* (2009); Aimee Meredith Cox's *Shapeshifters: Black Girls and the Choreography of Citizenship* (2015); Bettina Love's *Hip Hop's Li'l Sistas Speak* (2012) and *We Want to Do More Than Survive* (2019); and Monique Morris's

Sing a Rhythm, Dance a Blues (2019) and *Pushout* (2015), the latter of which details the ways in which Black girls' bodies are disciplined. Along with Aria Halliday's *The Black Girlhood Studies Collection* (2019), these texts create and represent an archive of creativity, celebration, and survival through dance, performance, and music in their own work. We cannot, however, separate the stories of violence and responses to trauma against Black women's and girls' bodies negotiated in many of these narratives and detailed in Treva B. Lindsey's 2022 *America, Goddam: Violence, Black Women, and the Struggle for Justice.*

Light and Legacies seeks to merge the politicized aspects of Black girls and, inviting more familiarity, a self- and community-designated "Blackgirl" existence, including visibility as a threat, as something that Black women writers have always taken seriously and addressed in their work. Before our "magic" was recognized as a hashtag, storytelling was our gift, alongside survival to tell those stories. From Phillis Wheatley's narratives of spiritual, if not physical, deliverance as poetry to Maya Angelou's revelation of "why the caged bird [still] sings," to Toni Morrison's illustration of what was but could never actually be the "bluest eye," words became the reclaiming of space, black letters on white pages that took up the space that these characters did not always have for themselves. Virginia Woolf's idea of a "room of one's own" became pages of one's own even as they were shared with the world, and the light and legacies these authors offered became what still guides Black girlhood today. Their stories of Black girlhood were, are, and will be lights that continue to shine from even the darkest places.

"love jones" for Nina S. of North Carolina

> To be young, gifted and Black, that's where it's at.
> —Nina Simone

Born Eunice Waymon in Tryon, North Carolina, musical genius Nina Simone is a local (at least to me, as a resident North Carolinian) designee of the light that shined from Black girlhood on. The Netflix documentary *What Happened, Miss Simone?* (the title comes from Maya Angelou's question, "But what happened, Miss Simone?" in a 1970 *Redbook* article) tells her story, in her words, of her journey from childhood pianist with dreams of being the first Black female classical pianist to international performer. She wanted to be in Carnegie Hall, and in 1963, she was, but not playing Bach. "How are you going to tell anyone who has never been in love how it feels to be in love ? . . .

But you know it when it happens." That love was for her family but especially for her music. Simone, who became known as the "High Priestess of Soul," stated, "I had a couple of times on stage when I really felt free . . . I'll tell you what freedom is to me, no fear. I mean really no fear."

As Waymon, Simone began to play piano at age three or four. Her mother was a preacher and took her to revivals, and she played in the church. "Revival meetings were some of the most exciting times that I ever had. . . . I was leading it." A White music teacher heard her and decided to give her lessons, and she studied with Mrs. Mazzanovich for five years, having to cross railroad tracks that separated Black neighborhoods from the white areas of town. Simone stated, "She was alien to me" but appreciated the teacher starting her on Bach in her desire to be one of the world's greatest classic pianists: "And this Bach, I liked him."

Waymon also became aware of isolation from the Black and white communities—they just wanted her to play piano for them to dance: "I was a black girl, and I knew about it [color]. . . . I lived in the South for seventeen years," she states in the film. Money saved for Waymon sent her to The Juilliard School for a year; the Curtis Institute of Music in Philadelphia initially rejected her admission for being Black. Her family moved north to be near her, and she got a job playing in a bar in Atlantic City, where she performed pop songs, classical music, and spirituals and was also told that she had to sing. Called "Nina" by a boyfriend and adding Simone professionally from French actress Simone Signoret, Nina's career developed quickly, as she was put on the Newport Jazz Festival lineup in 1960 and then recorded seven or eight songs. The public picked out "I Love(s) You Porgy" for acclaim, and she was then introduced by Hugh Hefner on the TV show *Playboy's Penthouse*, where she played the song, which launched and continued her very public career. Simone stated, "It was always a matter of necessity from day to day what I had to do. . . . I never thought about a choice" (a quote accompanied in the film by her song "It's Nobody's Fault but Mine").

Her only daughter is Lisa Simone Kelly, of whom Nina said, "I loved being a mother. I was a good mother . . . a goddamn good mother, and . . . the first three hours she was born were the most peaceful of [Nina's] life." Kelly said that her mother had a very lonely life because she practiced so much: "My mother was Nina Simone 24/7, and that's when it became a problem." Kelly adds, "She found a purpose from the stage, a place from which she could use her voice to speak out for her people. But when the show ended, everyone else went home . . . and she was alone with her demons" of anger and rage at the state of violence against African Americans in America. "She couldn't live with herself, and everything fell apart."

According to the film, Simone resented being torn away when Lisa was born, as she had to maintain a sense of normalcy for her daughter through constantly changing nannies and by other means outside of immediate family. She would also get extremely frustrated when her musical team wouldn't listen, as a friend stated: "She got into Carnegie Hall, and she got the big house in the country, but she began questioning herself."

After her song "I Wish I Knew How It Would Feel to Be Free," the film says that she was never able to separate herself from her work and social issues: "I never could quit because [her manager/husband] worked [her] too hard." The story is told that she was always "fighting, fighting, fighting," as her husband Andrew also physically abused her; in Simone's voice: "He was brutal, but I loved him. And I guess I believed he wouldn't do it anymore." Her daughter Lisa also adds, "She had this love affair with fire. . . . There was something missing in her, some meaning." Simone found that meaning in her work, as she stated, "I could sing to help my people, and that became a mainstay of my life," adding, "My job is to make them more curious about where they came from and their own identity and pride in that identity . . . mostly to make them curious about themselves . . . it's like a lost race."

The bombing in Birmingham, Alabama, on September 15, 1963, that resulted in the deaths of four young girls and the injuries of twenty others in the church was one of forty bombings in Birmingham at that time. James Baldwin talks about kids being murdered "and no one cares," and Simone's music directly responded to that and other incidents of violence against Black individuals and communities: "When the kids got killed in that church . . . that did it. First you get depressed, and after that you get mad"—she wrote "Mississippi Goddam" and played the Selma March on March 25, 1965, in Montgomery, Alabama, as marshals and military police surrounded them with guns, along with Langston Hughes and a number of well-known activists and performers.

In lyrics amended specifically for the March, Simone began, "Alabama's got(ten) me so upset, Selma [changed from Tennessee] made me lose my rest, But everybody knows about Mississippi Goddam," after which singing she got so angry that her voice was broken and never returned to its former octave, being full of rage. Simone begins the song, "The name of this song is Mississippi Goddam, and I mean every word of it," adding "I could let myself be heard about what I'm feeling about what I was feeling at the time." Lisa states that "Energy, creativity, passion" kept her going. From then, Simone became both part of and connected to the intellectual background of the movement. Langston Hughes wrote the lyrics to her song "Backlash Blues," and Lorraine Hansberry, whom Simone called one of her "best friends," coined the phrase "To Be Young, Gifted and Black," which also became the title of one of Simone's songs. Hansberry was her daughter Lisa's godmother. Betty Shabazz, wife and then widow of Malcolm X, lived next door and was like one of the daughters, to which Ilyasah Shabazz concurs: "These were brilliant, well-read, well-traveled" individuals. Her sister, Ambassador Attallah Shabazz, adds, "I'm born of the Young, Gifted, and Black" affirmation, as she describes how people would stand up and engage in a sense of African identities "without apology" when Simone performed.

Simone's involvement was her passion but also her calling, as she stated: "I'm one of those people who is sick . . . of the establishment, sick to my soul of it all . . . and it must be exposed before it is cured," also telling Dr. Martin Luther King Jr. that she was "not" nonviolent. "I thought we should get our rights by any means necessary." It was also a stressor, as she said, "I had to live with Nina. . . . Nobody is going to understand or care that I'm too tired. . . . Now I would like some freedom somewhere . . . where I didn't feel those pressures." She is described at that point of having "no control over her emotions," with mostly physical engagement (sex) underlying her relationship with her husband. Attallah Shabazz notes, "Participation and activism during the '60s rendered chaos in any individual's lives. . . . People sacrificed. Nina Simone was a free spirit in an era that didn't really appreciate a woman's genius. So what does that do to a household and a family . . . because of your soul not being able to do what you need to do?"

Hansberry died in 1965 from pancreatic cancer at age 34; Malcolm X was assassinated at 39 in 1965; King, also at 39 in 1968; and Simone said, "We can't afford any more losses," as the documentary quotes her singing "Why (The King of Love is Dead)" after King's death, "If you have to die it's alright 'cause you know what life is, cause you know what freedom is for one moment of your life." In reflecting on life in America after these impactful tragedies, Simon added, "I felt chased all the time, no matter what I did or how sad I got. I felt that there was just no life for me in this country." She decided to leave with a note, "I ain't got nothing to give, Andrew. And I'm too tired to even talk about it," adding that she was at peace "having as little to do with human beings as possible." Divorcing her husband Andrew, Simone decided to go to Africa to live, in Liberia, founded by formerly enslaved African Americans.

"It only makes sense that I should feel at home here," even wearing bikinis and boots as regular attire. "I also am keenly aware that I've entered a world that I dreamed of all my life and that it is a perfect world." The United States becomes "a dream that I had had and worked myself out of it . . . and now I am home, now I'm free."

Lisa moved to Liberia during her seventh-grade year and lived with a family until her mom came back. She states that Nina "went from being my comfort to a 'monster,'" physically disciplining her daughter and pushing her buttons in public. Lisa returned to New York at fourteen and never went back. Andy says that Simone began to live a nomadic life with no manager, lost the house, and stopped playing piano but had to pick up her career again, moving to Switzerland, where she performed at the Montreux Jazz Festival in 1976, beginning, "I'm tired. You don't know what I mean," and citing what others have said about her former stardom. "I hope that you will see me or see the spirit in another sphere, on another plane very soon now." Simone even interrupted her show, singing "Stars" by Janis Ian: "Stars, they come and go . . . like the last light of the sun all in a blaze. . . . But it gets lonely there when there's no one there to share." Simone added, "If you'll hear a story. . . ."

Simone continued: "They always have a story. . . . Now you must make way. . . . But you'll never know the pain of using a name you never owned/The years of forgetting what you know too well/That you who gave the crown have been let down/You try to make amends/Without defending." Nina Simone then left Switzerland and went to Paris, saying that she "landed in the wrong place." She stated in an interview, "I wouldn't change being part of the civil rights movement . . . but some of the songs that I sang have hurt my career . . . it's hard for me to incorporate those songs anymore because they aren't part of the times . . . There's no civil rights movement. Everybody's gone." She lived in a small apartment and was described by friends as "uncontrollable," dressing in rags. Simone's friend Gerrit moved her to Holland and brought in a doctor who prescribed her medication for manic depression and bipolar disorder, noting, "She got so deep in the shit that she realized it's either dying or give in . . . and she gave in." Lisa describes nervous tics caused by the medication Trilafon that also caused her abilities to decline, caused her voice to become slurred, and gave her mobility issues but allowed her to perform. This did not, however, Lisa notes, do anything for her heart and the loneliness she felt. Simone added, "My personal life is a shambles . . . everything has had to be sacrificed for the music." Moods remained unpredictable, but she regained connection with the international audience, stating "I have suffered," as she picked up the song "My Baby Just Cares for Me" as her "last chance" to tour and travel.

Her daughter Lisa states: "She was happiest doing music. I think that was her salvation. . . . When she sat at the piano her fingers could fly. She was an anomaly. She was a genius, she was brilliant, and that brilliance shone through no matter what she was going through. Even into her old age, she was brilliant." Here are stories of those both lost in light but also who found their light and their legacies in art and in music, and for whom light became their source.

Note on How to Be: A Blackgirl's Guide to Conduct

Repeating the lines, "I wish I knew how it would feel to be free," Nina Simone noted the pressure of staying in place as a Black child of the South (even having to cross railroad tracks that physically created the boundaries between Black and white communities) in her narrative of feeling restrained from childhood into adulthood. Repeated throughout African American literature, the conduct narrative is one of the earliest and most persistent tropes about Black children, including girls, and is not new but is a consistent narrative of survival. In *Codes of Conduct*, Karla F. C. Holloway writes of an interaction with a young boy in a credit union told by his mother to act his age and not his color, after which time he "kept to his place," and she continued to think about her own childhood. Holloway narrates:

Those words, whispered with an intensity only a black child understands, initiate a public behavior firmly attached to a conviction that our places in line are easily jeopardized. So powerful and persuasive was its pronouncement that, as children, we even conscripted it for our own use. It was an ultimate put-down—the closest we could come to calling someone a name (which we were taught not to do) without actually doing so. Reminding our chosen enemies, even subtly, they had a color (and that it was black) served a mean purpose—and a demeaning one. (4)

In this case, she recognizes the intensity of the whisper issued to command "proper" public behavior, because it is familiar within her own community narrative. From a place of protection that could also hold or be read as a place a trauma, Black children have been told to behave in order to stay alive, no matter how demeaning the purpose or reminder. Narratives of lynchings before and including Emmett Till in Money, Mississippi, in 1955 became warnings that being in the wrong place at the right or wrong time could be fatal.

Mildred D. Taylor's series that included *Roll of Thunder, Hear My Cry* tells the story of the Logan family—Cassie, the well-known young Black protagonist coming of age in a family that is led by her mother and her grand-mother while her father works away from their home. Her grandmother is the matriarch and the owner of the land on which they live; and her mother is an educator who keeps Cassie and her brothers "in line" for the purpose of survival but who stands up for their needs in their segregated school and in the community that threatens their existence. Cassie constantly navigates and negotiates what it means to continue this lineage but also to develop her own sense of identity. This series, which includes stories of friendship across racial lines and a matriarch-led family's fight to keep their land when others poison their well, cut their trees, and otherwise threaten their property and bodies and which ends in *All the Days Past, All the Days to Come*, with Cassie as an adult deciding her future while her brothers fight in World War II, is perhaps the most comprehensive recent representation of Black girlhood narratives, but it is certainly not the only one. As Cassie and her brother Stacey have to get off of the bus and walk the rest of the way toward their home, Taylor reminds readers of scenes of behavior as regulation not only in personal interactions but on public transportation as well.

Disciplinary narratives were also pervasive in growing-up stories about Black girls. Toni Morrison's *The Bluest Eye* (1970) and, later, *Sula* (1973) represent two well-known narratives of Black girlhood: first, the plight of Pecola Breedlove, who was raped and impregnated by her father and finds girlhood solace and a home (and, magically, "blue" eyes) with the MacTeer family; and, later, Sula Peace, whose friendship with Nel Wright is shaped and challenged by her desire to be something different from the women in her town of Medallion, Ohio. In 1970, the year Morrison published *The Bluest Eye*, society was transitioning from the Black Arts and Black Power movements that brought visibility to Black women's narratives. This period, however, was also a Black girl renaissance, with representations that included voices that had not been heard in a concentrated way since the late nineteenth century.

In 1970, Louise Meriwether also centered stories of Black girlhood in *Daddy Was a Number Runner*. The protagonist Francie Coffin's father started running numbers when he lost his job, and the whole family was involved: "Mother played the numbers like everyone else in Harlem but she was scared about Daddy being a number runner. Daddy started working for Jocko on commission about six months ago when he lost his house-painting job, which hadn't been none too steady to begin with" (21). She is also seeking respectability and visibility in her classroom as she says, "Mrs. Oliver, my homeroom teacher, didn't even bawl me out for being late as I slid into my seat. I was disappointed. Maybe she didn't like me anymore" (23). Finally, Francie is also negotiating what girlhood versus womanhood looks like in her day-to-day life.

Francie narrates: "I was in first-year junior high at P.S. 81 between St. Nicholas and Eighth Avenues, one of the worse girls' schools in Harlem, second only to P.S. 136 uptown. A brand-new baby was found flushed down the toilet at P.S. 136 last week. Nothing like that had happened at my school, at least not yet, but everything else did." (23). This suggests that Black girls are aware of what happens around them even before it is close to home. What is close for Francie, however, is the realness of violence where they are.

> Everybody was excited at school today. There was a rumor that Saralee and Luisa's gang was gonna beat up all the teachers who were failing them. That would be just about every teacher in the school except Mrs. Roberts. I don't think even Saralee, leader of the Ebonettes, would dare tangle with Mrs. Roberts. She taught us art and was the only colored teacher at our school and nobody messed with her. We didn't even take our magazines into her room, she was that tough. (23)

The context of the story reveals that the girls were just as violent as the boys, or trying to be, willing even to fight with all the teachers except for the only "colored" one, who was tougher. However, Francie's story also discusses the relationship between the gangs and what she has to navigate herself as she discovers her own path to womanhood.

> The Ebonettes were the sister gang to the Ebony Earls, the roughest street fighters this side of Mt. Morris Park. When the Earls warred with their rivals, the Harlem Raiders from uptown, blood flowed all up and down the avenue. When they weren't fighting each other, the gangs jumped the Jew boys who attended the synagogue on 116th Street or mugged any white man caught alone in Harlem after the sun went down. It got so bad that the insurance man from Metropolitan had to hire one of the Ebony Earls to ride around with him for protection when he made his collections. Yeah, the Earls were tough all right and the Ebonettes tried to be just as bad. (24)

Francie and her friends do hope that Saralee doesn't beat up Mrs. Oliver, who "was white-haired and looked like somebody's grandmother" (24). Their families try to regulate their behaviors as well. In arithmetic, "Almost everybody, including me, took out our love stories and true confessions instead. We didn't even try to hide our magazines in Miss Haggerty's class and she was so terrified she just ignored them," with Francie stating, "It was a good time for me to catch up on my love stories because Daddy wouldn't even let me bring those magazines inside the house. He said he didn't want to catch me reading such trash" (24). Ironically, school becomes a place to exert the behavior that she is not able to participate in at home, but the girls are also navigating their own existence as they try to find their own stories through the magazines they read in class. Francie's friend Luisa asks Miss Haggerty to "talk a little softer . . . I can't concentrate on my story" (25). Luisa also helps Francie figure out representations of sexuality among those in her community.

> Luisa was Puerto-Rican—white Puerto Rican—and was real pretty with her hair cut in a bob with bangs just like Claudette Colbert. Her running buddy, Saralee, was a burnt-brown color, with red hair, of all things. She was extra ugly. There was a rumor that Saralee was a bulldagger. I don't know if that was true or not but she was certainly rough enough to be a man. (25)

This narrative ties back to the violence that is perceived by women and can only be regulated by the ability to fight back, as Francie says, "Both of them were older than the rest of us because they got left back so often, and everybody, including the teachers were scared of them. They fought with razors and the Ebony Earls would beat up anybody that messed with their sister gang" (25). Her friend Sukie is still in elementary school after having been left back twice, so the ages represented in the educational space differ as well (26). From the fights Meriwether represents to Pecola Breedlove's/Claudia MacTeer's fight with Maureen "Dog Tooth" Peale when kids call Pecola "Black-e-mo," to Monique W. Morris's representation of the ways that Black girls are disciplined for behavior in educational settings, we see several scenes of Sofia's representation in Alice Walker's 1982 *The Color Purple* (made popular by actress Oprah Winfrey in the film directed by Steven Spielberg) and continued in narratives of Black girlhood throughout the canon of African American literature:

> All my life I had to fight. I had to fight my daddy. I had to fight my brothers. I had to fight my cousins and my uncles. A girl child ain't safe in a family of men. But I never thought I'd have to fight in my own house. (40)

We hold these narratives of fighting and surviving along with those of little girls (and women reflecting on girlhood) dramatizing and documenting their lives. We have the *Mama, I Want to Sing!* musical of 1983 and film of 2012 (with a number of narratives of Black girls living their dreams, if not always realized, through music), but we don't always think about that narrative of "Mama (or whoever holds a guardian role), I want to write." This book is a requiem for those whose voices were not heard and whose voices continue not to be heard. It is also documentation of the love and light that has been shared by the written word. Black girlhood holds remembrance, dramatizing and documenting different time periods, including enslavement (records, mortality rates, and even narratives of those who didn't die in spirit). It includes remembering the names of the four little girls who were murdered in the bombing at the Sixteenth Street Baptist Church in Birmingham in 1963—Addie Mae Collins (age fourteen), Cynthia Wesley (age fourteen), Carole Robertson (age fourteen) and Carol Denise McNair (age eleven)—as well as Sarah Collins Rudolph, then twelve years old, the sister of Addie Mae Collins who was severely injured, and those who are still undocumented in their existence or remains.[1] Black girlhood includes the stories of the Atlanta child murders told by James Baldwin in *The Evidence of Things Not Seen* (1985) and later by Tayari P. Jones in her 2002 novel *Leaving Atlanta*, reminding us that Jones herself was a child in Atlanta during that time. It tells the deaths of Black transgender women in Charlotte, North Carolina, where I live (including Monika Diamond, who was murdered in 2020) or in all of our home, country, and city towns and remembering that all Black girls and women do not get to tell joyous Black girlhood stories.

> *March 30, 2022 (My mama's birthday)*
> For the memories of *The Color Purple* (Broadway 2006)
> With my mama and my sisters
> I sat on the end
> Watching Celie sew her pants.
> For the times I put on my own
>
> One leg at a time

1. "Four Black Schoolgirls Killed in Birmingham Church Bombing," HISTORY, originally published February 9, 2010; accessed August 25, 2022. https://www.history.com/. Green, Molette, "'Fifth Little Girl' in Birmingham Church Bombing Tells Harrowing Tale," nbcwashington.com, originally published February 8, 2021; accessed August 25, 2022. https://www.nbcwashington.com/.

Wondering what color they would be

When I *really* grew up.—j. b. lewis

Black Girls Matter

Why do we look to stories about these girls at this moment? What is it about these lives that matter so much but appear so little in their full representations?

Drawing from Toni Cade (Bambara)'s *The Black Woman* (1970), in which then-Cade anthologizes political and social issues as well as ideas around identity, beauty, and nationalism, this book discusses representations of girlhood by African American women writers to claim community and a transition in their sense of agency and self-identification, from external to internal senses of belonging. I use the lens of what scholar and critic Mark Anthony Neal calls the "post-soul generation" perspective to reclaim texts that represent and include narratives about critical periods in African American history, from before and up to 1954 (the year of the *Brown v. Board of Education of Topeka* decision, which influenced the narratives of Black girls, safety, and inclusion in a racially oppressive nation state) to 2017, when Angie Thomas documented the initiation and participation of a teenage girl in a social movement to respond to the murder of her friend by the police, and even to the present day, which is, at times, tumultuous. The fiction, poetry, and memoirs analyzed focus on the power of girls—specifically, Black girls—to recognize themselves in media and culture.

The significance of representations of African American girls and social engagement in literature extends from the argument in my first book, *Freedom Narratives of African American Women*, that Black women writers in the nineteenth century saw and defined themselves as free (in mobility, access, and education) in a different way from how society saw and defined them. They used their narratives to hold a mirror image of themselves up to the world in a way that revealed more about their character, sense of self, and circumstances (social and political) than did the ability of others to tell their stories. *Light and Legacies: Stories of Black Girlhood and Liberation* argues that this self-recognition begins in childhood, as the girls represent play as social interaction, from Harriet Jacobs in the 1830s (represented in her 1861 narrative *Incidents in the Life of a Slave Girl*) to Starr Carter in Angie Thomas's 2017 novel *The Hate U Give*, as characters realize their own agency.

In this book, I continue the archive of representation of Black girlhood in fiction into the twenty-first century, which has not yet been done in literary studies, in an effort to provide a literary history of where this idea of what we now know as "Black Girl Magic" and its significance in American literature. There are critical moments that represent childhood even as early as the eighteenth and nineteenth centuries that begin the stories that narrate Black women's lives. Through anthologies such as Toni Cade's *The Black Woman* (1970) and novels such as Toni Morrison's *The Bluest Eye* (1970) and *Sula* (1973), among other texts, attention is being paid to how girls see themselves in literature and what they are learning from their parents, and specifically from their mothers. We can look at this Black (em)powered literature not as a beginning but as a renaissance of sorts of how African American women authors look to girlhood to think about self-construction, images, and ideals.

These novels and memoirs of Black Power written by women writers (which also go back to their childhoods) represent both cultural representations and fictional production during the 1960s to ultimately realize how moments of tragedy and resistance were presented by the media, including the bombing of the Sixteenth Street Baptist Church in what Dr. Martin Luther King Jr. described in his eulogy of them as "one of the most vicious and tragic crimes ever perpetrated against humanity." The narratives provide social analysis of the civil rights movement through the Black Power (and its cultural component, Black Arts) movements and feature prominent representations of Black childhood, with a specific focus on what is passed down to Black children—specifically, Black girls—about the world around them through media.

The book's introduction, "Remember: Requiem for Black Girls," begins with an account of narratives of Black girls lost to emotional, spiritual, and physical violence in the past several decades. Starting with 1955, which, as the late Ntozake Shange wrote, was "not a good year for little blk girls," and continuing through 1963 (the year of the bombing in Birmingham that tragically took the lives of four Black girls in an act of White supremacy) into the more recent present (2022, when the lives of Black girls turned women are still being taken in tragic acts of violence), I discuss the narratives that commemorate and remember their lives.

Drawing from the concept and histories of Black Girl Magic and the social impact of #SayHerName and #BlackGirlsMatter by the African American Policy Forum, I argue that we should talk about little girls in literature who help us think about what a reclamation of Black girlhood looks like and why, in addition to a context of social histories of Black girlhood and where and how they have been represented.

Chapter 1, "Imagine: Black Girlhood from Play to Possibility," examines thematic representations of Black girlhood, beginning with eighteenth- and nineteenth-century representations, including Phyllis Wheatley's poetry and Olaudah Equiano's representation of his sister (from whom he is separated by his own account in his memoir), and continues through texts such as Frances Ellen Watkins Harper's novella *Trial and Triumph* in addition to returning to her novella and novel, respectively, *Minnie's Sacrifice* (1869) and *Iola Leroy* (1892) to analyze the ways in which fictional representations of girlhood circulated ideals that connected to how Black women saw themselves as adults. Black women also reflected on these ideals in later texts such as Emma Azalia Hackley's collection of talks given to Black girls called *The Colored Girl Beautiful* (1916) and Charlotte Hawkins Brown's *The Correct Thing to Do, To Say, To Wear* (1941).

Chapter 2, "Dream: Poetics and Possibilities in Black Girlhood Aesthetics," discusses representations of girlhood before and during the Harlem Renaissance and by authors such as Zora Neale Hurston from her early fiction to her depiction of Janie in *Their Eyes Were Watching God* who, from girlhood on, looked for herself in men before finding her own true nature. The chapter looks at these representations of Black girlhood as preliminary to the civil rights period of the late 1940s through the *Brown v. Board of Education* case of 1954 and the crisis around Black girlhood and education that ensued (and that was represented by young agents of integration such as Ruby Bridges and the Little Rock Nine).

Chapter 3, "Move: Girlhood and Social Protest," discusses images of Black girlhood in protest and social movements that accompany images in literature. This chapter also discusses children's roles in movements, from the Children's March in the spring of 1963 in Birmingham, Alabama, to the integration of schools around the South, including Jo Ann Allen Boyce's narrative of integrating schools in Clinton, Tennessee, in 1956—before the Little Rock Nine were escorted into Central High School—chronicled in *This Promise of Change: One Girl's Story in the Fight for School Equality* (2019).

Other narratives of growing up in this time period include Ntozake Shange's *Betsey Brown* (1985), a "coming-of-age" story about a young girl who is forced to integrate schools in St. Louis, and two memoirs of the Black Power movement: Elaine Brown's *Taste of Power* (1992), which includes her account growing up in North Philadelphia in the 1940s and 1950s before her activism with the Black Panther Party, and Assata Shakur's *Assata: An Autobiography* (1987), in which she discusses growing up in segregated Wilmington, North Carolina, in the 1950s before repeated unfounded allegations in the 1970s that concluded in a conviction, imprisonment, and, ultimately, exile after the accusation of murdering a New Jersey state trooper (for which testimony against her has changed). In a discussion of what Langston Hughes referred to as "a dream deferred," narratives of what happens to Black girls' dreams connect Hurston's characters to those such as Beneatha Younger, the sister of Walter Lee in Lorraine Hansberry's *Raisin in the Sun* (1959). Beneatha dreams of going to medical school before her family's inheritance is lost by her brother.

Connecting past and present characters around what dreaming allows for Black girls, the chapter also discusses the aesthetics of Black girlhood in poetry such as Jacqueline Woodson's *Brown Girl Dreaming* to narrate experiences of civil rights struggles in the South (in this case, Greenville, South Carolina, where Woodson's grandparents lived) and moments of poetic liberation through play. These memories connect to discussions of activism in fiction and memoirs by youths in the twenty-first century, including Starr Carter's protest of the killing of her best friend in the 2017 novel *The Hate U Give*, by Angie Thomas.

Chapter 4, "Create: On Radical Creativity," discusses the return to historical narratives in Ntozake Shange's account of 1955 "not being a good year for little/blk girls" in *for colored girls who have considered suicide/when the rainbow is enuf*, performed and published in 1976 (and referring to integration movements but also connected to the deaths of Emmett Till and the Montgomery bus boycotts and the impact of all on Black girls), and prolific representation of issues in Black girlhood (including literacy; sexuality; and physical, sexual, and emotional abuse in both families and institutions) from the 1970s through 1980s. Citing Toni Cade Bambara, Toni Morrison's *The Bluest Eye* (1970) and *Sula* (1973), and Alice Childress's *Rainbow Jordan* (1982), I argue that these texts also insert family narratives and rewrite negative depictions of Black families, women, and girls featured in mainstream media in addition to instilling senses of belonging, positive image and identity.

Chapter 5, "Build: From Black Girl Magic to Afrofutures," returns to Toni Morrison's *The Bluest Eye* and Sapphire's *Push* (1996) to confront social issues that also become prominent in policy discussions of accommodations needed for youths to promote equity and social justice. As the texts discuss narratives of, and responses to, state violence and the ways in which educational systems do not always provide supportive environments, the readers become witnesses to the harms perpetrated against Black girls and, then, Black women. Drawing from postsurvival narratives that consider futures of Black girlhood, the chapter includes a visual analysis of Amy Sherald's painting *All Things Bright and Beautiful* and its unveiling in Birmingham, Alabama; Michelle Obama's analysis of her childhood in the South Side of Chicago; Tayari Jones's reminiscences of lost childhood and girlhood in her novels *Leaving Atlanta* and *Silver Sparrow*; and Beyoncé's 2020 visual album *Black Is King*, which features her own daughter, Blue Ivy, and a presentation of her song "Brown-Skin Girl," which connects the joy of childhood to journeys through womanhood. I return, then, to the premise from whence this appearance of "magic" (actually representations of endurance and resilience) actually emerges with the epilogue "Reading Play as Resistance," which considers the histories of Black childhood and play in connection with the significance of imagination.

This book asks the question, What do Blackgirl (combined for familiar representations of Black girlhood) narratives look like as described, illustrated, and representative of the fullness of their—or our—lives? How do they represent the creativity that is embodied in everyday actions? Furthermore, what are the Blackgirl stories that were and are still being told, and how do we hear them? It also includes stories of my own journey, stories of the activism of Black girls-turned-women, and fictional and nonfictional witnessing of Black girlhood narratives.

As a central question, I ask what is written in the stories and by the bodies of Black girls? From writing about them to the ability to tell stories themselves, how do their tools of what Mecca Jamilah Sullivan calls "radical self-expression" emerge? Sullivan argues, "It is only through the expressive technologies of the body—technologies that understand movement *as* language—that black women can fully touch each other and forge spaces defined by our disallowed pleasure, desire, healing, and joy" (92).[2] I argue that a similar theoretical framework emerges in Black girlhood stories as through dance, performance, movement, and play.

My aim is to tell a deeper story about Black girlhood that has not been told before. By using the select lives of Black girls, I expand on how we can offer a further examination into the creative lives and practices of Black girlhood. Black women writers take us into the interiority of Black girlhood, the sweetness of their joy, and the passion of their desires for expression, at times

2. Sullivan, Mecca Jamilah. *Poetics of Difference: Queer Feminist Forms in the African Diaspora*. Chicago: University of Illinois Press, 2021.

misread only as temper, anger, and frustration at the limits placed on them. With the process of "reading Black girlhood a'right" (to cite Frances Ellen Watkins Harper's *Iola Leroy*), I seek to offer insight into ignored representations and misnamings of the ways they move through the world as written by their older but no less reflexive selves.

On Reading and Radical Creativity, Especially for Young Girls

I recently opened a book that my fifth-grade teacher, Mrs. Victoria R. Rogers, gave me in February 1993, when I was eleven years old. In it, she inscribed, "You will always be my star student!" The book was *Children of Promise: African-American Literature and Art for Young People*, and it was the first anthology of my own people, but not the first book, I ever owned. I don't know if she knows this, but Mrs. Rogers, whom my children now call "G.G." (for godgrandmother—I'll add the fairy part), was also my first African American teacher at an integrated fine arts magnet school in Augusta, Georgia, which I attended from fifth grade until graduation.

I remember her telling us to "ask Mr. Webster" when we didn't know words, and I still tell my children, to check the dictionary for words that they don't know. I remember being Louis Armstrong for our biography project and bringing my dad's trumpet from his high school band class to school, along with a recording of "What a Wonderful World." I remember passing by her house one weekend, during the height of the COVID-19 pandemic, and her asking if she could still hug me as she gathered goodies for the kids. Mrs. Rogers is a living legacy for me and for my family. As my son now has now finished fifth grade and gone on to middle school, it is a blessing for both my children to know who taught me.

I reopened *Children of Promise* on July 14, 2020, in the summer after the COVID-19 pandemic re-exposed the social unrest that had been bubbling at the surface of Black America for decades. The foreword was written by Mary Schmidt Campbell, then commissioner of cultural affairs, New York City, and now retired president of Spelman College, the location of my first academic job as an instructor (before her tenure or position as president). Campbell says: "When Langston Hughes writes of 'our temples for tomorrow' or when Robert Hayden speaks of celebrating the life of Douglass, the life of the slave who reinvented himself, '. . . with the lives grown out of his life, the lives/ fleshing his dream of the beautiful, needful thing,' they remind us that as we strive toward that perfection, we are all children of promise." I am a child of promise who has come into a promising adulthood teaching the texts in this book. It is a reminder that we are a beautiful people who have continued to build foundations even when the ground is shaking under us.

The first text in *Children of Promise* is a poem by one of my favorite poets, Gwendolyn Brooks, from Chicago, Illinois (where I have lived as an adult). It is called "Building." Brooks writes: "When I see a brave building/straining high, and higher,/hard and bright and sassy in the seasons,/I think of the hands that put that strength together . . . ." She continues, "All little people opening out of themselves,/forging the human spirit that can outwit/big Building boasting in the cityworld." (Sullivan 6). I am not originally from a big city, but I know the spirit of buildings. I know the feeling of looking up at skylines even in my current city of Charlotte, North Carolina, and wondering just how a building can stand so strong.

The women and girls in *Light and Legacies: Stories of Black Girlhood and Liberation* were and are those buildings for young Black writers, including how I came across or remember their work and what their characters meant to me as Blackgirl herstories. You might name them differently, and I hope that the readers write stories of your own.

Introduction

Remember: Requiem for Black Girls

> We are involved in a struggle for liberation: liberation from the exploitive
> and dehumanizing system of racism, from the manipulative control of a
> corporate society; liberation from the constrictive norms of "mainstream"
> culture, from the synthetic myths that encourage us to fashion ourselves
> rashly from without (reaction) rather than from within (creation).
>
> —Bambara (7, *The Black Woman*)

> Our energies now seem to be invested and are in turn derived from a
> determination to touch and to unify. What typifies the current spirit is an
> embrace, an embrace of the community and a hardheaded attempt to get
> basic with each other.
>
> —Bambara (7)

I write this in summer 2020, summer of the death of George Floyd, of Iyanna Dior, of Nina Pop, of Tony McDade, of Breonna Taylor. I write this as a thirty-nine-year-old Black-identified woman. Thirty-nine was the age when Martin and Malcolm (names abbreviated for their extensive legacies) were murdered. Their wives lived much longer and continued to live with the burdens of their memories and of their lives.

I write this not knowing what it is going to be but including essays about Black girlhood and books that I wish I had known and read as a young Black girl. I invite voices that shape and influence me and current conversations about Black girlhood, too. These are histories, herstories, and our stories. But we are also still writing our stories and herstories and responding in our own ways to the ever-changing world we see.

I write this because people think that Black girls are loud, but at times I don't think we are loud enough. I write this because Zora and Angela and Toni and Audre (first-name familiarity out of love, not disrespect) were my "sheroes" before Beyoncé. I write this because Beyoncé (and me, and Black women and girls whose stories are here), all carry their legacy.

I write this because people are asking how to talk about what is going on in our world and because my daddy played me jazz on the way to school, where he drove me and my sisters every day on the way to his job at the hospital, where he saved lives as he treated and operated on people's hearts. But he also lost some patients, people who were special to all of their families and who mourned their losses just the same.

I write this in 2020 on the day that Sandra Bland died in 2015. She was twenty-eight years old. Sandra Bland was arrested during a routine, or "everyday," traffic stop in Prairie View, Texas. The assault on her body was recorded on camera, and she was found dead in her jail cell from asphyxiation, which means strangling or choking.

This is a book about Black women whose presence shone but also about those whom we have lost. Their lives and their spirits continue to light the way for each of us. Here are their words.

Sometimes I use the word "narratives" and sometimes I use the word "stories," but they are both ways that we know their lives.

Liberation is what my now twelve-year-old calls a "fancy" word for freedom, but it means something similar. Liberation is defined by Oxford Languages as either the act of setting someone free ("from imprisonment, slavery, or oppression") or "freedom from limits on thought or behavior." We can think about freedom from limits as the legacy that many of these writers and authors offer. How do they make it possible for their characters, and for their readers, to live limitless lives? Each story features a "telling," points for discussion, and sometimes even questions. I hope that anyone reading this book will learn about the authors' lives and the stories they told but also be inspired to tell new stories, more stories, and stories of their own.

Dedication II, My Soft Black Song

Refrain: In the first grade, I won my first contest, which was a poetry contest. My teacher was Mrs. Parker, a sweet, older (at least I remember her as being older, although she may have been my current age then) white woman from Lexington, Kentucky. For every poem we memorized, she let us put a black dot on our paper ladybugs. The person with the most dots won the prize.

Although my memory is terrible now, I remember that I had been practicing Shel Silverstein poems with my best friend from kindergarten (who now is mother to a high school senior—crazy!) on the phone. There's no telling how many times we went back and forth reading *Where the Sidewalk Ends*, and I'm sure now that most of my poems came from that book. I don't know how many dots my ladybug ended up having, but I remember fondly and still have my prize from that contest—Nikki Giovanni's *Spin a Soft Black Song*.

The summer after eighth grade, I was selected for Duke University's Talent Identification Program (TIP), and it was my first trip to Duke (where I would later spend four years), four hours, but what seemed like a lifetime, from my hometown. It was my second summer doing TIP. The previous summer, I took philosophy, which I thought was the same as psychology, wanted to come home, and came up with some paper about the brain. But that second summer, I took "Introduction to African American History," taught by a Black woman poet, Camille Dungy, who continues to write beautiful work. I also met my now-famous poet friend Alexis Pauline Gumbs in that summer seminar. We spent the summer reading texts from a big anthology called *Crossing the Danger Waters*, analyzing racism in popular films (including the *Lion King*, pre-Beyoncé), and choosing research projects to study in the library.

I had done one research project in my eighth-grade year, and it was on the Black Panther Party. I don't remember how I chose the Panthers, but I spent weeks making catalog cards with indexed topics (the system before Google) and learning about the Panthers' Ten-Point Program. So that summer, filling in all the blanks that my Georgia public school education had omitted was magical for me. My project was on the four little girls who were murdered in Birmingham, Alabama, on September 15, 1963. My mother was eight years old at the time and living in Athens, Georgia. She would have been around the age of some of the children in the Sixteenth Street Baptist Church at the time of the bombing. My daughter, now eight, came to know and learn this story, which still resonates powerfully.

In high school, Zora Neale Hurston was the light that guided my writing, as I read her during the same year that I lost my grandmother Vanilla Bowman (who was a lifelong educator). In Mrs. Franklin's AP English Class, we took apart the language of *Their Eyes Were Watching God*, but what stuck with me was Janie Crawford's grandmother trying to protect her from the world by marrying her off. Before her marriages, though, Janie spent time outdoors waiting for her own life to bud like nature. I was waiting, too, and wrote every college and scholarship essay on the book and Janie's relationship with Nanny. To my memory, it is the first and only novel I read by a Black woman author in the curriculum, but I found Toni Morrison's *The Bluest Eye*, *Sula*, *Jazz*, and *Tar Baby* on my mother's shelves at home (along with Terry McMillan's *Disappearing Acts* and *Waiting to Exhale*, which I brought to Friday reading in seventh grade, and my teacher, Ms. Berger, never batted an eye). I remember reading both James Baldwin's *If Beale Street Could Talk* and Morrison's *Paradise* in my high school's library, checking them out again and again until I finished both (and sometimes reading more than once).

When I went to college at Duke University four years after that summer and a year after reading those Hurston essays, I worried for just a second that I would not have the influence of Black women writers around me. I was wrong. One of my first English classes was Dr. Charlotte Pierce-Baker's "Designs for Black Women's Living." We read everything in that class from *ESSENCE* articles (I would have the amazing honor of being named one of *ESSENCE*'s "Ten Incredible College Women" three years later) to another text I still have and hold dear, Audre Lorde's *Sister Outsider*. That class taught me not only that Black women's lives were sacred texts but also that we had always told our stories even before other people misrepresented who we were.

It is these experiences that inspire my writing today as I teach college students African American literature and—surprise!—Black women's writing. My first book, *Freedom Narratives of African American Women*, focused on their freedom stories from the nineteenth century to the turn of the twentieth century, but I will do some recap here for a different audience. This book is for the legacies of those earlier lights. *Legacy* means something passed on or inherited, and if these texts speak to you, or even if you have to come to know them, they are for you.

Each chapter highlights an author (or several), their work, and their stories. It is a book for reading, thinking, and working. I hope that readers come to know and love these stories, too. Chapter titles both speak to the theme of the narratives but also represent mandates to continue the work that the writers initiated with Black girl characters. I begin these writings with a dedication by my own daughter who made me both reflect and play, before and during the shut down during the spring of 2020 because of the COVID-19 virus and pandemic. Time together encouraged us to exist deliberately and, collectively, to remember our stories.

I. Remembering Stories, Written with Delany Lewis, at Age 7

This story is for the four little girls (their names are cited earlier) who were killed at the Sixteenth Street Baptist Church in Birmingham, Alabama, on September 15, 1963. This story is also for my little girl. She had just turned seven in the summer we mostly stayed home because of the COVID-19 pandemic, which still challenges us in 2022. But before in-person school ended in March, she learned a lot at the University of North Carolina at Charlotte, my home institution where I teach. She met Dr. Angela Davis when Dr. Davis was invited to speak in February 2020, just weeks before the entire country and the world shut down because of COVID-19 and people began to respond (again) to Black lives not mattering enough in America. When I told my daughter who Dr. Davis is and that she was born in Birmingham, Alabama, Delany asked me if Dr. Davis knew the four little girls (whom Delany knew from touring the Civil Rights Museum in Atlanta in January). She told Dr. Davis when we took her back to the airport that she wanted to write a book about her, and here we are.

We did more research, and Delany, a budding speller, wrote then that the four little girls are "Who angala daveses mom tot when they where little ["Who Angela Davis's mom taught when they were little"]." She is right. Bloody Sunday in the United States, on Sunday, March 7, 1965, marked the march of six hundred people out of Selma, Alabama, on US Route 80 who were attacked by state and local lawmen wielding tear gas and billy clubs on the Edmund Pettus Bridge only six blocks away. They were turned back toward Selma as they walked for their civil rights (maybe even singing hymns for strength and resilience). Almost two years earlier, on September 15, 1963, four African American girls were murdered at the Sixteenth Street Baptist Church in Birmingham by a bomb planted by White supremacists that also injured several others. Many Americans don't say the names of Addie Mae Collins, Cynthia Wesley, Carole Robertson (three fourteen-year-olds killed in the bombing), and Carol Denise McNair, age eleven, the only one whose murderer Robert Chambliss was tried and convicted (of first-degree murder twelve years later), although the FBI concluded investigation in 1965 with the naming of four well-known Klansmen and segregationists. After that cold case was revived by the state, two others were convicted of four counts of murder and sentenced to life in prison in 2001 and 2002, and a fourth died before ever being charged.

Angela (as Dr. Davis was known then) was from Birmingham but away at Brandeis University when the four little girls were murdered by White supremacists (those who believe their whiteness gives them power to harm) who planted a bomb at their church. I came to know Dr. Davis's work, first as an eighth grader when I wrote my first research paper (which was on the Black

Panther Party) and then as a college student at Duke University in a Black theory course that used *The Angela Y. Davis Reader*. Dr. Davis also wrote in response to the fifty-year commemorations of the bombing of the Sixteenth Street Baptist Church and Dr. King's *Letter from a Birmingham Jail*, "What I fear about many of these observances is that they tend to enact historical closures. They are represented as historical high points on a road to an ultimately triumphant democracy; one which can be displayed as a model for the world . . . ." (64).

In *Freedom Is a Constant Struggle* (2015), Davis noted, "We think individualistically, and we assume that only heroic individuals can make history," adding that Dr. King "was a great man, but in my opinion his greatness resided precisely in the fact that he learned from a collective movement. He transformed in his relationship with that movement" (pp. 118–19). Davis has also been part of many movements. The HistoryMakers, the nation's largest African American oral history archive, talks about Davis's life as an activist, author, and professor. They note her activity in the Black Panther Party and the Communist Party; her formation of an interracial study group and volunteering for the Student Nonviolent Coordinating Committee while still in high school; and her continuing on to study in New York, Germany, and Paris before attending Brandeis University, where she graduated magna cum laude, and then earning her master of arts degree in 1969 from the University of California, San Diego, in 1968 after additional study in Germany.

The HistoryMakers archive notes that, after becoming an assistant professor at the same institution, Davis was then removed because of her connections with the Communist Party and the Black Panther Party. After her dismissal, she worked to free the Soledad Prison Brothers and, in the process, befriended George Jackson at Soledad. She was then put on the FBI's Most Wanted list after he and several other inmates attempted escape from the Marin County Courthouse in August 1970, despite the fact that, as the HistoryMakers note, "she was not at the crime scene." Davis spent eighteen months in jail during her trial and was acquitted in 1972, after which time she continued her life's work of teaching, speaking, and activism. While in prison, Davis wrote *If They Come in the Morning: Voices of Resistance* by hand and was hired by San Francisco State University after her acquittal. Davis ran on the Communist Party ticket for vice president of the United States in 1980 and 1984.

After teaching at San Francisco State University for twelve years, Davis taught in the History of Consciousness Department at the University of

California, Santa Cruz. Davis also co-founded the Committees of Correspondence to connect and unite Socialist groups in the United States. She wrote several books detailing her experiences, including *Women, Race and Class*, *Are Prisons Obsolete?*, and *Freedom Is a Constant Struggle: Ferguson, Palestine, and the Foundations of a Movement*. In the foreword to the latter book, Dr. Cornel West calls Davis "one of the few great long-distance intellectual freedom fighters in the world." In addition to documenting movements for Black freedom, Davis continues to write and speak out against state violence, racism, economic and social apartheid, and liberation. In response to the violence that took place in her hometown and partnership with continuing struggles for freedom, Angela Davis is a living testimony to radical resilience and radiating light.

Davis's story leads into the purposes of this book: First, how do Black women writers, scholars, and activists use their stories of girlhood to discuss their pathways to liberatory practices; and furthermore, how do they create spaces of light and liberation for Black girls and other women?

Narratives of Black girlhood discuss how families and educators instilled messages of Black empowerment (even before the social movement) into Black children, and girls in particular, but also how African American women authors created and revealed their own sources of power by representing Black girlhood (their own or others) in their narratives. Although this is a literary project, it cannot be separated from other cultural narratives, including media representations and publications of the late 1960s through the 1970s, including those for the "new" Black middle class in the 1970s, which, Mark Anthony Neal argued in his book *Soul Babies*, emerged in television shows and films that represented African American or multicultural families. Parallel media include the introduction of *Sesame Street* on PBS in 1969 by the Children's Television Workshop and *Reading Rainbow* from 1983 to 2006. I am also arguing for an organic sense of Black feminist nationalism presented through print publications and media that reclaims Black girlhood both as a response and as a continuance of national/international resistance to oppression and misrepresentation.

The framework for the book includes both words and concepts that serve as themes in the texts but also as directives for how I theorize Black girlhood. As I begin, I want to elaborate on three central principles that have become the theories from which this book emerges. They are: Live, Shine, and Play. Although they are not the only ideas on which I, and they, focus, without them, none of us or this study would exist.

II. Live: On Resurrecting Black Girlhood

I would like to view blackness as a measure of how *all peoples* in the United States construct an intimate idea of self in relationship to the nation—by having, in that little corner of their imagination a black seed against which all action—and therefore in the existential sense, all being—is differentiated.

—(Holland 16)

Anything dead coming back to life hurts.

—(Amy, *Beloved*)

In *Raising the Dead*, Sharon Holland writes that "Raising the dead became a figurative enterprise, as well as an intellectual and therefore concrete endeavor. The task was both to hear the dead speak in fiction and to discover in culture and its intellectual property opportunities for not only uncovering silences but also transforming inarticulate places into conversational territories" (4). Drawing from Toni Morrison's speech "Unspeakable Things Unspoken: The Afro-American Presence in American Literature" and her novel *Beloved*, Holland continues to think about the "unaccomplished imaginative shift from enslaved to freed subjectivity *and* the marked gap between genealogical isolation and the ancestral past [which] form the meeting place where the bulk of [her] ruminations on death and black subjectivity reside" (15). If we go to these silences, inarticulate places, marked gaps, and meeting places, what might we find about ourselves (as Black women and communities) and reveal about our Black girl selves?

Furthermore, how do we recenter Black girlhood as a narrative from which others emerge as a narrative of nation? Can the nation be one that begins at the beginning, with girlhood, instead of, or even in addition to, being projected back upon? To return to the epigraph, can Black girlhood be the seed of imagination from which all being emerges? Holland argues that categories "in which liminal subjects can reside and from which they can speak," including terms created by critics and authors "like *marginality* and *invisibility* to aid those outside of master narratives and places of power in articulating a politics of experience," can be empowering at times "but it also can be mercurial and dangerous." She challenges relegating our experiences to margins, stating, "as intellectual constructs, theories of the margin hold much promise, but as paradigms for what it is like to be marked as black in this nation, they fall short of the mark. The experience of being in the margin is much like that of skating on thin ice" (16). Much of the rhetoric around Black girlhood seems to be just that—marginalized spaces, troubled territories, skating on the thinning ice between girlhood and womanhood. So where, then, can we articulate experiences of Black girlhood beyond the margins, beyond invisibility, and as central to the nation? How, to continue with spatial analysis, can we bring what is "outdoors" inside?

In Toni Morrison's *The Bluest Eye*, Pecola Breedlove is "outdoors," having been placed in the MacTeer home after her father's physical abuse of her mother and sexual abuse of her leaves her family without a stable environment. As Pecola stays in the MacTeer household, Claudia's narration of Pecola places her in a more supportive domestic environment, from Frieda MacTeer helping Pecola when her menstrual cycle begins to the girls being part of her school network as well (along with Maureen Peal, who becomes a source of sore response when Claudia becomes jealous of Maureen buying Pecola ice cream).

Holland theorizes "outdoors" in Morrison's *The Bluest Eye* as a space of dying:

> In her paradigm, outside becomes "outdoors," and peripheral existence or marginal space describes a living death—a full embrace of the concept of death. Here "outdoors" is synonymous with being dead. To resist outsider status, to come back from the dead, is a monumental existential feat in Morrison's world. There is no full embrace of the margin here, only the chance to struggle against both a killing abstraction and a life-in-death; neither choice is an appealing option. (17)

After wishing for (and believing she gets) blue eyes, Pecola is ultimately left further outside of social expectations of redemption. Holland, however, pushes us to theorize that loss rather than relegating it to beyond our sphere of understanding:

> For those beyond the periphery, beyond even a language of the margin, for those literally "outdoors" and therefore dead to others, there needs to be a theory profound enough to explain such a devastating existence. . . . The impending task is then to define, in as much as possible, the vehicle used by authors writing about traditionally marginal(ized) experiences to speak and to legitimate the power of that discourse. (18)

This, perhaps, is the theorization from which we begin. We go to the dead, to the dying, to explain the "devastation" of their existence. We ask them what happened, what is happening, and how to prevent the reoccurrence of the cycle. As Holland argues, "We must investigate the viability of theoretical examinations of the margin in the context of the articulated experiences of those who seem to dwell in what Morrison calls an abstract existence" (18), which suggests that we have gotten our understanding wrong.

Through texts such as *Lose Your Mother* and *Wayward Lives*, Saidiya Hartman reclaims the existences of girls on the slave ships through the lives of the women in the Harlem Renaissance. Black feminist theory, especially since the 1980s, has expanded the territory from which we can explore self and selfhood for Black women. This trope for Black girls has been examined and reclaimed through music (Bettina Love's *Hip Hop's Lil' Sistas Speak*), performance (Aimee Meredith Cox's *Shapeshifters*), and games (Kyra Gaunt's *The Games Black Girls Play*). By looking at literature, we see the ways in which the Black women writers in this study seek to reclaim the lives before the emotional and, at times, even physical deaths by representing Black girlhood as lived.

From eighteenth-century poetry through nineteenth-century fiction and into memoirs and fiction of the twentieth and twenty-first centuries, the women in this study represent life, light, and legacies of the power and strength of their endurance and existence. I end, and therefore begin, with this from *Raising the Dead*: "The dead embody, and therefore become so much of, what the living are unable to realize" (19). Black womanhood is able to exist is when Black girlhood dies, literally and figuratively, but girlhood may be resurrected as well. Once that resurrection of girlhood exists, the next paradigm, "shine" can as well.

III. Shine: Black Women and Play

When asked about her signature poem "Ego Tripping," Nikki Giovanni said she wrote the poem because she came up on oral narratives like "Shine," which celebrated Black male braggadocio but left no space for Black girlhood. In an interview with Pearl Cleage ("An Evening with Nikki Giovanni" for the HistoryMakers in June 2005), Giovanni stated, "I'm tired of little girls 'looking to the east and west for somebody to love,'" as she referred to the chant "Little Sally Walker, Sitting in a Saucer."

In connecting her stories of growing up in the South, Giovanni describes one incident when her grandmother signed her up to picket after the Birmingham bombing, stating that she (her grandmother) was "too old" but that Nikki was an appropriate age. This became a lesson to her: "If there's one thing my grandmother did for me, I knew there was no safety," in addition to the many lessons shared by her grandmother, for whom she wrote the poem "For a Lady of Leisure, Now Retired" when she died. Giovanni's poem states, "there are so many new mistakes/for a lady of pleasure/that can be made it shouldn't be/necessary to repeat the old ones," with the lesson "if I never lost I wouldn't have appreciation for what I've won." Losing becomes a reminder to preserve what has been gained, both in people and in experiences.

Giovanni's story of her college years at Fisk University, one of her great lessons, includes wanting to go back to Fisk to "correct [the] failure" of getting expelled." She went back on her own terms, talking to the new dean of women, because she and the former dean "had different visions of what a lady should be." She asked for an apartment so as not to live on campus with the college-age girls, to which the dean agreed. Because she was able to maintain her sovereignty even while fulfilling the requirements of the institution, she is able to remember and refer to Fisk as an "important important institution."

These lessons are what she refers to specifically in that interview, and in other conversations, in equally important ways. One example is *Parks v. La-Face Records*, filed for Rosa Parks against the duo OUTKAST for their song "Rosa Parks" (refer to the lyrics, "Ah, ha, hush that fuss, everybody move to the back of the bus), in which she says they missed an opportunity to teach. Giovanni states: "Somebody had to bring it to Rosa Parks' people and they brought it the wrong way. We have to teach future generations who the[se people who came before them] are." I read this to mean that older generations have to take the responsibility to teach those who come after them the lessons they have learned. The messages passed down through generations are to know and acknowledge who built and sturdied the ground on which we stand but also how subsequent generations continue to solidify that ground.

In her lens as a Black woman shaped by both race and gender, Giovanni states, "I look at the world as a Black woman so I'm always writing through that," noting that she is "a Southern Black woman very much grounded in the women of my grandmother's generation. . . . Our socialization has been different because so much of our youth was spent in public." However, much of what has been publicized about Giovanni's generation, which emerged in a public sphere with the activism of the 1950s and 1960s, also, connects to the race and gender lenses of more contemporary periods. For example, acknowledging the legacy of Tupac Shakur in her work has been one of the examples of Giovanni's connection across generations, as she states, "It is not right for the old to bury the young," and continues, "This generation mourns Tupac as our generation mourned Emmett Till."

Giovanni, the mother of a son, states that she "cried as all mothers cry" on learning of Tupac's death. But in an extended dialogue, she also acknowledges the complicated legacy of Shakur and other rappers who may represent less than favorable language or lyrics about Black women.

In describing the effect of their lyrics, she expands that girls "are not feeling excluded . . . not feeling an attack by what he's saying," which connects to the study and writing about girlhood and hip hop in books such as Dr. Bettina Love's *Hip Hop's Lil' Sistas Speak* (2005). Although these connections are further theorized in the work of Aria Halliday and other critical scholars in Black girlhood studies, it is important to note that Giovanni's connection of her own activism in writing and in the media to the generations, including the lyrics that become the legacy of the 1990s and the 2000s as well, continue in her interactions with those who came into the spotlight after her.

When given the opportunity to do an interview with Queen Latifah, Giovanni flew to California to her, rather than vice versa, saying "she was busy, and it was my turn to not be busy." She recounts telling Queen Latifah, "I am supposed to be there for you." This is exactly the idea of connecting light and legacy—bringing lessons that one has learned to generations that need them.

This trope was not new in the late twentieth century but instead was instilled in conduct literature from the nineteenth century into the mid-twentieth century, when women such as Emma Azalia Hackley (author of *The Colored Girl Beautiful*) and Charlotte Hawkins Brown, founder of the Palmer Memorial Institute (Sedalia, North Carolina) and author of *The Correct Thing to Do, to Say, to Wear*, offered instruction for young women in educational settings. These lessons, and creating environments of support so those after them could "shine," are part of Black women's legacies.

This book and the lessons therein are dedicated to the lights and legacies of Zora Neale Hurston, Gwendolyn Brooks, Nikki Giovanni, Alice Walker, Elaine Brown, Assata Shakur, Toni Morrison, Maya Angelou, Ntozake Shange, Sapphire, Jacqueline Woodson, Tayari Jones, Angie Thomas, and other elders who have told their stories and stories of Black girlhood. Their stories are for all of us.

IV. Play: Dreaming Black Girlhood: Play as Past, Present, and Future

A third paradigm is where play comes from in African American life and culture. With the tragic loss of actor Chadwick Boseman in August 2020 during the ongoing pandemic that began in winter, earlier that year, the cry and posts of "Wakanda Forever" have circulated throughout the globe. I remember taking my two children and meeting their friends at the local theater, which is still closed because of the COVID-19 global pandemic. A photograph of that moment taken by my friend and colleague brought back so much: Moving through the world freely, watching kids see themselves on the big screen, and seeing not just Boseman as Black Panther but also Letitia Wright as Shuri (who actually made the use of the vibranium possible and created the key to Wakanda's technology success through Prince T'Challa's outfit) revealed the real secrets to #BlackGirlMagic and the magic of Black children as well.

Although #BlackGirlMagic is a more recent hashtag-turned-movement, popularized as such in 2013 by CaShawn Thompson and linked policywise to the African American Policy Forum's work to support Black girls (and the memorializing of their lives and struggles through #SayHerName), scholars and practitioners of dance, literature, music, drama, art, and so on can document Black girls' abilities to navigate the world through not just human resilience or innate strength but also creativity and imagination.

Shuri represented sisterhood but also innovation within a familial unit. She was a loyal daughter, supporting her mother when T'Challa got to be the face of the community. In the comic book based on her name (by Nnedi Okorafor), we see Shuri representing all of these things as she displays STEM (science, technology, engineering, and mathematics) prowess with humor and care. She, in addition to T'Challa, is a representation of what manifests when Black children, even in imagined worlds, are able to dream and are supported in their efforts. To use the language of feminism for Black girls, Shuri's journey involves learning to move throughout the world as a girl and then woman, seeing her mother as a lead figure in policy after the death of her father, and working along with her brother to create a stronger society for Black people.

Shuri also, however, represents the playfulness of creating for Black women: As she is responsible for making the products with vibranium, she jokes with her brother about her own capabilities that enable his. Her creativity enables her to respond to the demands of her people with calmness, humor, and competence. Although a fictional character, she is an image of futuristic prowess that exists in her present, all in a Black woman's hands. In the idealized image of Wakanda, she makes it possible for her brother to bridge the legacy of rule in their family (under the guidance of their mother). Play enables her to realize her ability from the past to the future.

A Note On Play

In the *Child's World of Make-Believe*, Jerome L. Singer describes the research of Karl Groos in 1901, in which Groos proposed that "play emerges out of natural selection as a form of necessary practice on the part of the child or immature organism for behaviors that are essential to later survival. In this sense, the playful fighting of animals or the rough and tumble play of children and many of the playful courtship activities of animals and children as well are essentially the practice of skills that will later aid their survival" (p. xxxiv). The survival skills that each of these authors are negotiating are those that secure their freedom. Make-believe for Harriet Jacobs as a child, for example, turns into her ability to negotiate spending seven years in her grandmother's cramped attic space awaiting her freedom and then playing the role of a sailor in order to escape to freedom. The ultimate goal, then, is the ability of "play" to help the restricted subject learn how to *live*.

Additionally, Inge Bretherton refers to Jean Piaget's 1962 notion of "play" as an "essential part in the development of operations . . . that alone make the coherent representation of reality possible" in her essay "Representing the Social World in Symbolic Play: Reality and Fantasy." Hence, pretending only continues so long as the child cannot effectively accommodate to the real world."[i] In texts written by such noted authors in African American history as Frederick Douglass, Harriet Jacobs, and Booker T. Washington, children's play is discussed as a means of negotiating the social hierarchy of enslavement. These texts, which are either directly situated within or connected to the genre of slave narratives, also present games as a means by which enslaved children were made to rehearse their future roles as adult slaves.

Through play, as Bretherton cites Piaget, children begin to form their adult identities and gain a greater understanding of their social status. In some cases, however, these narratives demonstrate how play occasionally allowed enslaved children to transcend the social hierarchy associated with slavery. Play provided them a space where they could manipulate social rules and assume, at least temporarily, the identities of free people. In a sense, play made it possible to make the transition from "enslaved" to "free," first in consciousness and even later in action.

Chapter 1

Imagine

Black Girlhood from Play to Possibility

In *Scenes of Subjection*, Saidiya Hartman specifically analyzes the vexed notion of "play" as it relates to activities in which enslaved persons participate, as she discusses the ambivalent nature of pleasure in captivity. I argue that interpretations of a constructed reality then led to "assimilation" to an actual reality and the demands that accompanied that reality. For example, Frederick Douglass understands himself as first a "child" and then a "man" in each of his narratives. This transition relates not only to age but also to a feeling of control over his identity. This framework of the restrictive nature of pleasure also comes from Douglass's analysis of holidays as "the most effective means in the hands of the slaveholder in keeping down the spirit of insurrection . . . as conductors, or safety-valves, to carry off the rebellious spirit of enslaved humanity" (75). Without them, he argues, slaves would give in to desperation. In this text, slave masters are both initiators of and partakers in this degradation—they play the "game" of freedom on the slaves, only to remove any possibility of a victory for the other players.

Defining Child's Play in Narratives of Enslavement

Narratives of the culture of play extend from the earliest known African American narratives through civil rights–era narratives and into the modern period. Imagined freedom and actual freedom are connected through a pattern first identified under an oppressive institution and into the restrictions of rural southern and even urban play. The traditions and ways of looking at play as not only escape but also transformation are critical; play has continued to have a role where the processing of development is related not only to adulthood but also to childhood, where play "begins" as well. Play serves as confirmation, modeling, and, eventually, transition into a world in which the narrator has the ability to comprehend and, ultimately, escape the ways in which he or she is objectified.

Historians often discuss the roles of men and women under the institution of slavery, but the plight of children (before they have come into defined gender roles as we understand them) is discussed less often. Perhaps this is because, in many cases, there was no differentiation between an adult male and younger male or between an adult female and younger female. At a certain age, they were expected to perform the same labor, whether those duties were located inside or outside of the home. In some slave narratives, however, the author locates himself or herself by a certain age, and that age generally denotes a transition in consciousness. Although the list of "coming-of-age" narratives of slavery is not conclusive, texts that have become established narratives of gender and enslavement in the African American narrative tradition also discuss these shifts in understanding of one's social status.

Play narratives are not new, especially in diasporic literature. In *The Interesting Narrative of the Life of Olaudah Equiano, or Gustavus Vassa, the African* (1789), Equiano describes his transition into slavery as one that removed him from a culture of play in itself. After offering an account of his country that included customs and traditions, buildings, religion and a culture of war, and ceremonies and superstitions, Equiano describes his own family trajectory that allowed him to engage in child's play before he and his sister were captured. His father owned his own slaves, and Equiano writes that seven of the children "lived to grow up, including myself and a sister, who was the only daughter" [x]. Equiano notes, "As I was the youngest of the sons, I became, of course, the greatest favourite with my mother, and was always with her, and she used to take particular pains to form my mind" [xi]. This description of the intellectual development offered by his mother is in addition to the assistance she gave him in a male-dominated warrior culture. He continues: "I was trained up from my earliest years in the art of war: my daily exercise was shooting and throwing javelins; and my mother adorned me with emblems, after the manner of our greatest warriors. In this way I grew up till I was turned the age of eleven, when an end was put to my happiness in the following manner" [xii]. Note here the description of adornment as a kind of physical confirmation of greatness. However, the culture of play is still one in which he is instilled, as the narrative continues. Equiano offers this description of "play culture":

> When the grown people in the neighbourhood were gone far in the fields to labour, the children generally assembled together in some of the neighbours' premises to play; and some of us often used to get up into a tree to look out for any assailant, or kidnapper, that might come upon us. For

they sometimes took those opportunities of our parents' absence, to attack and carry off as many as they could seize. [xiii]

This passage suggests not only that kidnapping was regular but also that guarding against it was part of a "game." He notes that the grown people were laboring while the children "played" and that both children and adults knew that kidnapping was not just a possibility but a regular occurrence. Although Equiano goes on to give "alarm" of one of his peers who was almost kidnapped, he also states that "[A]las! Ere long it was my fate to be thus attacked, and to be carried off, when none of the grown people were nigh" [xiv]. Again, his distinction between adults and children is important here because, as a child, he did not have the duties that would keep him away from the home.

He describes the removal from his home as such: "One day, when all our people were gone out to their work as usual, and only I and my sister were left to mind the house, two men and a woman got over our walls, and in a moment seized us both; and without giving us time to cry out, or make any resistance, they stopped our mouths and ran off with us into the nearest wood. Here they tied our hands, and continued to carry us as far as they could, till night came on . . . ." [xv]. This passage actually begins Equiano's narrative of enslavement, at which point they were "then unbound, but were unable to take any food" [xvi]. The inability to eat is a recurring trope throughout the narrative. But another point of significance, which is generally not discussed in scholarship about this text, is that it represents the captivity of a male child and a female child, as Equiano describes himself and his sister.

As he comes to a personal understanding of how they are being treated and what they are not allowed, he also presents a picture of physical restriction that he witnesses his sister endure. "[M]y cries had no other effect than to make them tie me faster and stop my mouth; they then put me into a large sack. They also stopped my sister's mouth, and tied her hands . . . ." [xvii]. Equiano understands immediately that the loss of his voice, which he attempts to use to notify travelers of his capture, is not the only "problem." His sister's voice is taken away as well. These scenes reveal the power of speech and action that women also had in his Igbo culture. Equiano continues this narrative by analyzing the culture of captivity. He writes that "the only comfort we had was in being in one another's arms all that night, and bathing each other with tears. But alas! We were soon deprived of even the small comfort of weeping together. The next day proved one of greater sorrow than I had yet experienced; for my sister and I were then separated, while we lay clasped in each other's arms" [xviii]. This is the moment in which Equiano reveals an understanding of what enslavement actually means. He is first separated from his family, then silenced, then separated from the only person who remains familiar to him. But, I argue, that Equiano's narrative is also that of his sister, who remains without voice except for what he offers. If his story is tragic, so, also, is hers, as we lose her story when they are separated.

Tropes of gender and the culture of play are extended in narratives of the nineteenth century through Douglass and Jacobs. In the beginning of his *Narrative of the Life of Frederick Douglass* (1845), Douglass also chronicles his life of enslavement (born to an enslaved mother and a father that, only by myth, may have been his master) from infancy. He writes: "My mother and I were separated when I was but an infant—before I knew her as my mother. It is a common custom, in the part of Maryland from which I ran away, to part children from their mothers at a very early age. Frequently, before the child has reached its twelfth month, its mother is taken from it, and hired out on some farm a considerable distance off, and the child is placed under the care of an old woman, too old for field labor" [xx].

Douglass's knowledge of slavery, specifically in Maryland, where he begins his narrative, starts as an acknowledgment of the separation that the institution requires. Douglass suggests that because of the desire to prevent family connections, the child is not allowed to be "mothered," even as he or she is "cared for," which is another way of securing value for the child's master. This reflection moves from theoretical to personal, however, as Douglass continues: "For what this separation is done, I do not know, unless it be to hinder the development of the child's affection toward its mother, and to blunt and destroy the natural affection of the mother for the child. This is the inevitable result" [xxi]. In this stage of understanding, the suggestion of what the rupture can do turns into a realization of the inevitable result: destruction of any kind of connection that could have created a different consciousness of a child. In Douglass's case, his mother assumably has to fend for herself, even as she tries to parent from a distance. We do not get her narrative either or what she endures in the institution of enslavement.

Douglass's mother's story is a narrative of girlhood that is disrupted and even interrupted as he centers his story. Douglass also notes the loss of independence and play as a potentially revolutionary activity in his 1855 narrative *My Bondage and My Freedom*. He repeats, "But the majority spent the holidays in sports, ball playing, wrestling, boxing, running foot races, dancing, and drinking whisky; and this latter mode of spending the time was generally most agreeable to their masters . . ." but he adds "fiddling, dancing, and 'jubilee beating" as ways in addition to games that the enslaved persons can speak out against their situation in addition to participating in the fun enforced by the masters [xxviii]. Enforced play was originally categorized for Douglass in the same way as dancing and drinking—as a waste of time when compared with the more industrious tasks that slaves could complete for their own benefit. Being made to play instead of being allowed to control their free time was both disappointing and deceitful. However, adapting rules of play into their own performances later becomes a means of resistance rather than of restriction.

We look to the present and to the past to see from whence theories of Black women's play emerge. The analysis of play in both an understanding of and transition into freedom is also present in *Incidents in the Life of a Slave Girl* (1861). Harriet Jacobs writes, "My mother's mistress was the daughter of my grandmother's mistress. She was the foster sister of my mother; they were both nourished at my grandmother's breast. . . . They played together as children; and, when they became older, my mother was a most faithful servant to her whiter foster sister" [xxix]. Play, in this instance, is what demonstrates to Jacobs both the connection and the division between her enslaved mother and her mother's mistress. Although both women were nursed by Jacobs's grandmother—her mother's mother—and both played together as children, raised almost as sisters, age would then establish the division between slavery and freedom, as her mother becomes her mistress's servant.

In her relationship with her own mistress, Jacobs writes that her mistress was kind and would even sew by her side. She states, "When she thought I was tired, she would send me out to run and jump," again positioning play as a "break" from labor [xxx]. However, Jacobs quickly iterates that "Those were happy days, too happy to last" as she then divulges a narrative of attempts to escape sexual abuse from her master as she approaches her fourteenth year. [xxxi] For Jacobs, "play" is also an imitation of freedom once she learns that the reality of slavery, first for her mother, and then for her, sets in.

Jacobs's life is divided into the period before and after the age of fourteen, which she defines as the point when her master recognizes her as a woman. She is then unable to continue to "make-believe" in the same way as before, because reality destroys her play. Jacobs uses "play" to identify problems such as not being the same color or having the same social status as her young mistress, which she must then negotiate in real life (first within the institution of slavery and then through a quest for actual freedom). Analyzing the cultures of play, specifically among girls-turned-women, offers an alternative to the narratives of vulnerable womanhood that represent the genre. A modern context connects the ability of both men and women to see how play allowed them to work through circumstances of restriction and oppression. An understanding of instrumental play provides readers of these texts with the tools to explore the possibility of transcending slavery that was realized even before the authors' narratives turned toward freedom. These moments set up the audience for understanding the narrators' desires for and realization of freedom. Furthermore, play serves as a rehearsal for freedom, as it allows the narrating subjects to make sense of the world.

Hartman discusses this negotiation of enslaved bodies to subjugation through physical labor and amusement:

> Generally, the response of the enslaved to the management and orchestration of "Negro enjoyment" was more complex than a simple rejection of "innocent amusements"; [r]ather, the sense of operating within and against these closures made the experience of pleasure decidedly ambivalent . . . pleasure was less a general form of dominance than a way of naming, by contradistinction, the consumption and possession of the body and black needs and possibilities. [iv]

In this assessment, pleasure is used to control by possessing Black bodies. However, it also seems to allow that leisure can be a way for Blacks to repossess their bodies from those who dominated them by the same means.

Bretherton argues: "Pretending simulates and transforms routine events from family life, storybooks, and television. . . . However, the ability to represent these scripts (and their distortions and transformations) does not emerge fully fledged" [v]. Although this analysis incorporates a contemporary media framework, it still addresses the ways in which the subject must transcend the gap of representation. Douglass, for example, cannot "become" the master of his own fate without developing an understanding in closer proximity to a culture of enslavement than his childhood consciousness allows. However, his immediate consciousness (at least in reflection) is one of what enslavement prevents, which is connection to his actual family and inability to grow up in a culture of sanctioned child's play.

Collectively, all of these narratives illustrate examples of the "rhetorics of play" discussed by Brian Sutton-Smith in *Ambiguity of Play*. Specifically, the rhetorics of play as "power," "identity," and "the imaginary" theorize the very ways in which these narratives understand and engage the culture of play.

Sutton-Smith defines the "rhetoric of play as power" as being "about the use of play as the representation of conflict and as a way to fortify the status of those who control the play or are its heroes" [vi]. The "rhetoric of play as identity . . . [is] usually applied to traditional and community celebrations and festivals [and] occurs when the play tradition is seen as a means of confirming, maintaining, or advancing the power and identity of the community of players" [vii]. Sutton-Smith argues that "The rhetoric of play as the imaginary, usually applied to playful improvisation of all kinds in literature and elsewhere, idealizes the imagination, flexibility, and creativity of the animal and human play worlds" [viii].

These various definitions cover both the "orderly play of girls in their folk games" and the "play of disorder: games of chance, of symbolic inversion, of carnival, of 'deep play,' as well as the 'games people play, 'war toys,' playfighting, play therapy" [ix]. Reading play in narratives of enslavement as a negotiation of social hierarchy, as a means of confirming and advancing power and identity, and as a way to connect the imagined to the actual world can help the reader to understand how these texts become a means of understanding and promoting their authors' versions of freedom. Playing roles allows narrating subjects to understand and foresee realities that are alternate to the ones that they endure. Collectively, these texts demonstrate ways in which play serves as regulation on one hand and as a transition to liberation on the other hand. In each perspective, the significance lies in both who holds and who can interpret the instructions, rules and regulations; that is, the means to "win."

Extending Play into Contemporary African American Culture

I hearken back here to Zora Neale Hurston, whose dreams led to the representation of her characters Isie Watts and Janie Crawford, in her short story "Drenched in Light" (1924) and her novel *Their Eyes Were Watching God* (1937), respectively. Isie wants to go along the road to Orlando and watches the cars as they pass by, adding her own adventures to her grandmother's chagrin. Janie wants to realize the strength and power of her own budding sexuality but instead starts her journey toward womanhood by marrying a much older man of her grandmother's choosing for her protection. She then spends much of her life as a wife or partner before finding liberation both within and outside of relationships on her own terms. Her connection is also to the South, to land, and to her own spiritual environment. Hurston creates characters that play and pursue their dreams, but at times these dreams are delayed because of race and gender.

Ideas of connection to environment and the turmoil that living through racial unrest can bring to a young girl, along with the power of familial support, are the cornerstones of Mildred D. Taylor's Logan Family Saga series, which includes books from *Song of the Trees* in 1975 to *Roll of Thunder, Hear My Cry*, and continuing to *Let the Circle Be Unbroken*, *The Friendship*, *The Well*, *The Land*, *The Road to Memphis*, and the most recent book with protagonist Cassie Logan as an adult, *All the Days Past, All the Days to Come* (2020).

Likewise, Jacqueline Woodson's 2014 *Brown Girl Dreaming* discusses the stories of connection between the protagonist's family in Ohio and maternal grandparents in Greenville, South Carolina. She reflects how her father never wanted to go south because of the (extant) racism but how she desired the southern and extended family connection even when she had to see her grandparents subject themselves to racist behavior. Woodson's text, along with the others, draws from the tradition of Black family narratives established as early as, if not earlier than, Frances Ellen Watkins Harper's nineteenth-century accounts (in poetry, speeches, and fiction) of Black women's experiences. Of particular interest is *Trial and Triumph* (1888), in which a young girl, Annette, is taught the values that make her a "good" girl, unlike her parents who departed from lessons of respectability. Annette really just wants to enjoy life, which leaves her, like Hurston's Janie Crawford, outside of the protection of her family. All of these narratives allow us to think about support within family structures but also how, and what happens when, Black children play.

Stories of Play

Even some of the most memorable moments in my childhood involved learning and passing down repetitive hand-clapping games. Most were accompanied by singing and, at some times, other bodily movements. The most popular children's hand-clapping song that I remember, "Miss Mary Mack," is also one on which I can find little documentation or history. Some sources suggest that perhaps the song is named after the USS *Merrimack*. Other sources cite the song as "unknown" or just as a common street game. Joanna Cole and Stephanie Calmenson discuss the song in *Miss Mary Mack and Other Street Rhymes*, suggesting a perhaps more urban element to the story of Mary Mack "all dressed in black/with silver buttons/all down her back." However, I remember learning the song in two different versions—one was from my mother, who was raised in a southern town in north Georgia, and the other was from classmates, as I was raised in a different small city in a different part of the state. The versions only differ slightly, and there are dozens of similar songs and games that define "play" for African American childhood communities, but this reflection connects thematically and contextually to the ways that the cultural significance of play is defined for African American boys and girls through centuries of slavery and into freedom.

Theorizing play in Black girlhood involves looking at spaces in which Black girls interact, sometimes evident in public spaces (for younger and even older children)—playgrounds, yards, and streets—but it can also mean looking beyond the public eye to spaces such as rapidly changing social media platforms, from visual performances on Snapchat to the dances currently included on TikTok (which I'm sure will continue to change with evolving technologies). Except for their primarily digital components, these interactions are not altogether different, however, from the handclapping games discussed by Kyra Gaunt in *The Games Black Girls Play*. We also, however, have to look at the playfulness of Black women, the laughter, the coded talk understood internally (wordplay), and even their own memories of play. From the original idea of play as mockery, rules are set in place to regulate the participant's ability to challenge repressive aspects of society. In all of these narratives, however, play is used to negotiate identity, power, and even respectability.

We also, however, use Black girlhood to project a future of play. The following chapters discuss poetics and possibilities in the aesthetics of Black girlhood (Ntozake Shange's *for colored girls who have considered suicide/when the rainbow is enuf*); representations of games and play in texts of the 1940s and 1950s (Gwendolyn Brooks's *Maud Martha*); and play as resistance, as represented in Shange's *Betsey Brown* and Toni Cade Bambara's *Gorilla My Love* and documented by Harry LeFever, even as games played in jail for those imprisoned in civil rights protests. Through texts such as Louise Meriwether's *Daddy Was a Number Runner* (1970), returning to Morrison's *The Bluest Eye* (1970), and also adding *Sula* (1973) to Alice Childress's *Rainbow Jordan* (1981), I look at play as negotiations of democracy and nationhood, with the intersections of girlhood and Black Power to Black empowerment. This work examines images and identity, and where these Black girl protagonists find the sources of their light.

Chapter 2

Dream

Poetics and Possibilities in
Black Girlhood Aesthetics

Oh Jesus, make me wonderful!
—Nel Wright, *Sula*

W hat does it mean to be a "Colored Girl Beautiful" (i.e., what does a Black girlhood aesthetic look like)? In 1916, Emma Azalia Hackley published *The Colored Girl Beautiful* as E. Azalia Hackley, author of "A Guide in Voice Culture" and "Public School Lessons in Voice Culture." Hackley dedicates the book with the following words: "To colored women in whom I have faith and to colored children whom I love, I send this little message." Initially, beauty seems to be defined as behavioral, but Hackley constructs her instructions out of love, as she compiled the volume from talks given to girls in "colored boarding schools," beginning at Tuskegee Institute by request of the dean of the Girls' Department. These talks served as examples of initiatives sought for support to educate girls at largely male institutions out of attempts to represent their beauty, both internally and externally, and regulate proper behavior.

Hackley wrote, "It was an impromptu talk after an hour's notice. Just before the Dean closed the door to leave me alone with the girls, I repeated my question, 'What shall I talk about?' The reply was, 'Tell them anything you think they should know. They will believe an experienced woman like you who travels and knows the world and life'" (9). She continued, "As I looked at the sea of faces, 'wanting to know,' and as I thought of all they had to learn, the vastness of all of it almost overpowered me'" (9–10). In this moment, Hackley realized her power to give the girls a platform to talk about anything "that is interesting to every one of [them]" (10). The "heart-to-heart" talk that followed covered answers about "love—real love" and "beauty—real beauty" in an informal way.

Hackley stated: "For forty minutes we had a heart to heart talk. The dean and teachers had perhaps told the girls the same words, but the message seemed to come more directly to them from one who had daily contact with the great, busy world" (10). As she spoke, she thought of the idea that similar talks might be given to girls at other schools. "Then came the request, 'You come so seldom, can you print the talks?' Much of the talks could not be printed because many of the questions and answers were personal'" (10–11). She concluded, "If I had a daughter I would desire that she should know these things and more, that she might be a beacon light to her home and to the race. As I have not been blessed with a daughter, I send these thoughts to the daughters of other colored women, hoping that among them there is some new thought worthy of a racial 'Amen.'" (11). The thoughts Hackley hoped for also represented what will make the girls *beacon lights* to their homes and to the race. She desired that they serve as examples for the rest of their community, both the educational community and those looking to them to model intellect and access.

Looking for a racial "'Amen'" to Hackley looks to me like Hurston's project of claiming identity through Janie Crawford in her 1937 *Their Eyes Were Watching God*. Janie, the main character, had to learn to be excited about being herself, and then her grandmother married her off to a much older Logan Killicks for her own protection. She then stayed in a series of marriages and relationships before she came back to her hometown of Eatonville, Florida (a real place) to be with her friends. The question of what might come out of exploring your own identity is a good one, too. Sometimes deciding our destiny isn't completely in our hands, but there are others to support our dreams.

I return to the story of Harriet Jacobs, who was born into the institution of enslavement in Edenton, North Carolina, in 1813. Jacobs's story begins in childhood, watching her mother serve her own white sister until her early death, seeing her brother not be able to go to their father when also called by their master, and becoming subject to her master's advances before reaching adolescence. Critics such as Sharon Holland have argued that Jacobs had to adopt her own notions of freedom to substitute for the lack of consent that she actually had in her life. She arranges her own path to freedom (which her grandmother opposed, ripping away her mother's wedding ring when Jacobs confesses her first pregnancy), having to endure time enclosed in a space in which she could not even stand (but which she imagined and knew would be better than the experience of enslavement from which she came).

Desire for aesthetics of right and righteous behavior, at least as others could see, regulated Jacobs's grandmother's thoughts about her behavior. Even though she knew that enslavement at the hands and whims of the Norcom family, especially Dr. Norcom (named Dr. Flint in the book), prevented her granddaughter from living the pure—or, at least, consensual—life she would have desired, she remains aware of what others think of her choice to go outside the household to pursue her own path to freedom.

After bearing two children fathered by a white politician—and finding that their births did not, as she had she expected, free them from a predatory master and jealous mistress—Jacobs escaped to a garret in her grandmother's attic in Edenton, North Carolina, where she remained for seven years, subject to seasonal elements, vermin, and a paralyzing lack of physical movement. Painful representations of what Jacobs's family suffered and the emotional and physical violence committed by the Norcom family who enslaved her make the horrific events and the audacity of the freedom dreams she depicts in *Incidents in the Life of a Slave Girl* seem incredible. Indeed, Jacobs's book (published under the pseudonym Linda Brent) was read as fiction until research by Jean Fagan Yellin definitively established the veracity of Jacobs's story and authorship. Jacobs did not see those before her model physical freedom, as her mother died when she was a child (and, as a daughter, Jacobs couldn't even attend to her). She saw her grandmother try in vain to buy her children. Her grandmother's dream was for her own children to be free and to create their own legacies.

In many previous and subsequent narratives, Black girlhood is represented by dreams of maternal or matriarchal figures. Frances Ellen Watkins Harper's novella *Trial and Triumph* and her novella and novel, respectively, *Minnie's Sacrifice* (1869) and *Iola Leroy* (1892), describe Black girls' desires to be free from judgment, to marry and/or parent (or not), to choose their own careers (including that of an intellectual, as Harper chose), and to live as free women.

Hurston's *Their Eyes Were Watching God*, perhaps one of the more well-known stories of dreaming, began in 1937 with Janie Crawford's dream of selfhood that comes, as Jacobs argued, "not through marriage," although Crawford marries multiple times. However, it also doesn't come in Jacobs's way either, through children, as the fictional Janie does not have any. Janie's freedom comes by dreaming her own pathway, which departs from her grandmother's initial desire for her to marry for her own protection and then through two unsuccessful marriages, a courtship that ends in her partner's death by rabid dog and then gun, and a return to the friendship circle that birthed her.

I have long been fascinated, even a bit obsessed, with the line in Zora Neale Hurston's *Their Eyes Were Watching God* in which Janie reflects on her return to the town of her younger womanhood (Eatonville, Florida) and declares that her tongue is in her friend Pheoby's mouth. Colloquial for the idea that her friend knows her well enough to tell the story, this statement also suggests a more personal knowledge of Janie's life than the reader can perceive from the male-identified relationships that we often focus on. Janie's physical story moves through three husbands (Logan Killicks, Joe Starks, and Vergible "Tea Cake" Woods), but Pheoby is a "friend of her mind" as well.

After initially marrying the much older Logan Killicks to satisfy her grandmother who wants her to be protected, Janie goes to Eatonville initially with the founder of the town, Joe Starks, and returns as an older adult after Tea Cake's death. Her relationship with Pheoby, however, is a girlhood knowing that she did not have even when growing up. Early in the story, Janie reflects not on childhood friends but on the absence of her self: "So when we looked at de picture and everybody got pointed out there wasn't nobody left except a real dark girl with long hair standing by Eleanor. . . . Ah don't see me. . . . Everybody laughed, even Mr. Washburn . . . don't you know yo' ownself?" (9). Indeed, Janie didn't know enough about *her self* to see herself. The joke and the reason why everyone laughs are both because she does not stand out in the picture as a "real dark girl" and because she doesn't recognize her own face.

In Hurston's representation, Janie already knew that she was different before she dreams of her own inner sanctuary under a pear tree. As Janie looks at a picture of herself and sees the "real dark girl with long hair standing by Eleanor," her classmates laugh because she doesn't see herself at all. Finally identifying her image, Janie realizes, "Aw! Aw! Ah'm colored! . . . But before Ah seen de picture Ah thought Ah wuz just like de rest!" (9). Because she has been blending in with others, in personality if not appearance, Janie seeing herself as others see her raises the questions of how Janie comes to see herself through others.

Her aesthetics of self are defined by looking at others, by being "just like de rest" instead of her own unique being. She is described as the "real dark girl with long hair" because hair becomes another thing by which she gains approval or disdain. Other moments in the book note that Janie's critical second husband, Joe Starks, requires her to keep her hair up and invisible, and others' remarks on her appearance are based on her hair. Additionally, Janie sees beauty outside (of windows, on horizons, and in nature) that remind her of what true beauty is and means.

When Nanny sees Janie kissing Johnny Taylor under the pear tree, only an external manifestation of what Janie has already felt inside, and when Isie's grandmother sees her perched on the gatepost in an effort to leave domestic spaces for freer pastures up the road in Orlando, we see how what E. Patrick Johnson calls "quare" dreams of Black girlhood are represented. Johnson notes in his definition of "quare":

> On the one hand, my grandmother uses "quare" to denote something or someone who is odd, irregular, or slightly off-kilter—definitions in keeping with traditional understandings and uses of "queer." On the other hand, she also deploys "quare" to connote something excessive—something that might philosophically translate into an excess of discursive and epistemological meanings grounded in African American cultural rituals and lived experience. (126)

What we don't see in more restrictive definitions of queerness as strangeness (hence the use of quare) are the restrictions on these desires in spaces deemed private, dark, and not publicly celebrated, especially in southern spaces where narratives of Black childhood abound. Janie can only represent and celebrate her desires for freedom outdoors in public spaces, and these are also the spaces that others can see and restrict her activity.

Although Hurston illustrates Janie's childhood as one of coming into her own identity, this identity is not shaped in common with other children's identities. Before meeting and then returning to Pheoby years later, there is no group of girlhood friends represented in Janie's life. It is Johnny Taylor (and, specifically, the restrictions placed on Janie's sexuality) who becomes the reason for Janie's first marriage to the much older and more financially stable Logan Killicks. After her second marriage, to Joe Starks, her relationship with Pheoby, who remains Janie's "kissin'-friend for twenty years" (6), allows her to expand her representation beyond partnership with, or possession by, a male figure. For her southern communities, this expansion into a girlhood circle (or even relationship with a singular figure who is not a spouse) seems both excessive and irregular for one who should aspire to be a good wife.

Janie moves through the world and, specifically, through the natural world in a way that is different. It takes the natural "golden dust" of pollen to turn Johnny Taylor into an object for Janie's desire. Even their exchanged kiss does not compare with how Janie engages her own sexuality. On the one hand,

Janie's version of not being "jus lak de rest" (9) might release her from the expectation of blending in. This realization takes her outside of traditional circles of friendship into a "blossoming pear tree in the backyard that . . . stirred her tremendously'" (10). Janie's dream then is to leave the fixed frame of the class photo—where the expectation is to blend in—for the inner spaces of a free Black girlhood, where she experiences the transcendence of her body into a desire for something else, something better. She both wants to blend in (and even be surrounded by a circle of friends) and stand out by having a unique experience that transcends ordinary girlhood. This opportunity comes through Janie's connection to nature, to outside southern spaces of Florida in springtime. Under her grandmother's near-watchful eye, Janie "saw a dust-bearing bee sink into the sanctum of a bloom; the thousand sister-calyxes arch to meet the love embrace. . . . Then Janie felt a pain remorseless sweet that left her limp and languid" (11). She wishes "to be a pear tree—any tree in bloom" and wonders, "Where were the singing bees for her?" (11).

On the other hand, Janie still must pursue traditional pathways of marriage to fulfill others' desires for her regulation. Janie wants, and only gets, to see the world outside of the land that Nanny and Logan Killicks designate as safe spaces for her, with men and through the legal construct of masculine protection, an idea that is continued through subsequent marriages. The marriage to Logan fixes her domestically to the land she is made to tend with him. She then moves to Eatonville with Joe and is fixed in domestic spaces—both their home and, more publicly, the store—for decades until his death. After venturing onto "da Muck" with Tea Cake, which ends tragically for him and for their relationship, Janie comes back to Eatonville in a reverse migration to reclaim not only her physical childhood space but also her youth.

Hurston also represents an excessive physical location as she centers Florida, Hurston's designated home state after being born in Notasulga, Alabama. For Janie, the trees bloom in excess. Her pain, described as "remorseless sweet," is excessive for others as well, and every time she reveals aspects of her femininity (including the length of her hair, which is quickly covered up by Joe Starks's demands), she is pulled back within social boundaries. Even with Tea Cake, Janie is too much, and one instance of violence in which he slaps her is an attempt to trap her in regulated womanhood. Janie's exploration of her own identity first with others and then with her idea of a "kissing friend" (even metaphorically) represents the ways in which she first embraces then resists the containment of a regulatory would-be patriarch and continues to dream as she moves throughout southern spaces and physical locations.

Janie's longevity in memory is through her friendships and not, through the usual way, with marriage or children, as Janie states, "Pheoby, we been kissin'-friends for twenty years, so Ah depend on you for a good thought" (6).

The beauty represented here, both individually and by way of locale, is through southern spaces that drip beyond regulation as nontraditional aesthetic representations—for Janie Crawford, Eatonville and then "the Muck" become central locales of Black aesthetics. One is a space of building and progress; another, a space of fear, natural disaster, and death. Hurston's other characterizations of southern experiences provide equally complicated aesthetics —in her first short stories, there is John Redding in "John Redding Goes to Sea" (1921), whose "queer notions" of wanting to see the world leave him impaled on a wooden stake while helping to build ships; and Isis "Isie" Watts in "Drenched in Light" (1924), who sits on the gatepost and watches the cars drive off to Orlando, much to her grandmother's chagrin.

Isie's desire to leave the rigidity of her grandmother's domestic space to see the world up the road in Orlando and beyond echoes John Redding's queerness, represented as wanting to leave a space of defined masculinity for a place with unknown repercussions for African Americans. Isie climbs up the gatepost to watch cars going up the road, doesn't want to stay in the house; uses her grandmother's new tablecloth as a skirt, which she drags through the mud on the way to a dance; and begs a couple who is passing by to take her away so she won't be punished (they, in turn, talk to her grandmother and offer to take her anyway). Stories that focus on Black girl figures often model the supervision of a family or a matriarchal figure, who try to protect girls from the dangers of growing up Black in spaces that don't celebrate Blackness.

These representations are not isolated to Hurston's work, but they also connect to Toni Morrison's migratory narratives of Black girlhood to Lorain, Ohio, where Pecola wishes for blue eyes (a trait that exceeds the normal appearance or identification of Black girlhood to change what she is able to see) and Sula and Nel's "quare" friendship in The Bottom of Medallion, Ohio. In the lives of the women in *The Bluest Eye*, girlhood migrates from southern spaces to pervade every inch of the text and across class spaces as well.

Even upper middle-class women such as Junior's mother Geraldine (whose cat Junior throws violently to frighten Pecola) move from Aiken and Mobile to Ohio and also represents travel from rigid to fluid, seemingly more beautiful spaces. Pecola's dream for blue eyes, the bluest eyes, in front of which people won't do "ugly things," is also represented as excessive, as the ability to make and realize her own dream is her only escape from the fixedness of poverty and abuse. The magic of the eyes is transformative for her, even if only she believes that she has received them. The arguments that these examples and these texts make in a larger canon of Black girlhood are that girlhood spaces—specifically, the dreams and desires realized within them—represent a different model of being. Pecola's eyes are an example of the aesthetics that Black girls (and women) search for that appear to make the world more beautiful even when it is the same behind the illusion.

Beauty, here, is also tied to behavior and regulation. Janie's and Isie's grandmothers, Nel's mother Helene in Morrison's *Sula*, and even Mrs. MacTeer of the family who takes Pecola in are examples of the maternal figures who seek to protect their girls from racism, harassment, and social abuse. Hurston and Morrison also, however, incorporate African American notions of a "queer" childhood and how the dreams of girlhood are themselves quare. Isie's desires for both physical and social mobility as a girl deem her different and render Hurston's representation of southern girlhood as a particularly queer enterprise. Janie's attraction is not specifically to Johnny Taylor but to the potential to bud under the pear tree and to explore sexuality outside of a heterosexual framework and along with the natural occurrences of blooming taking place.

Black girlhood becomes already queer—or, as E. Patrick Johnson would call it, *quare*—as Isie's and Janie's desires for their own self-realization replace their desires for romantic connection. Hurston's designation of Black girlhood as particularly different raises the questions of how Blackness connects to quareness and, particularly, "quare" southern spaces such as Florida in Hurston's representations of Black childhood. Isie is willing to get dirty for play as she goes in the mud with her grandmother's tablecloth as her skirt. Although Hurston illustrates Janie's childhood as one of coming into her own identity, Janie also not have childhood friends. As a matter of fact, the only person we see her interact with is Johnny Taylor in a quasi-romantic way.

Years later, Pheoby, Janie's "kissin'-friend for twenty years" (7), represents the queer and, to draw from E. Patrick Johnson's notion, "quare" representation that deems Black girlhood already subject to a different field of analysis. Janie reflects on returning to Eatonville that her tongue is in her friend Pheoby's mouth. Colloquial for the idea that her friend knows her well enough to tell this story, this statement also suggests a more personal knowing of Janie's life than the reader can perceive from the male-identified relationships on which we often focus. Janie's story is one of the three husbands (Logan Killicks, Joe Starks, and Vergible "Tea Cake" Woods), but Pheoby is a friend of her mind as well.

These representations of dreams and desires as outside the ordinary are not isolated to Hurston's work but also connect to Toni Morrison's migratory narratives of Black girlhood to Lorain, Ohio, where Pecola wishes for blue eyes in *The Bluest Eye* to change what she is able to see and Sula and Nel's "quare" friendship in The Bottom, Ohio. The arguments that these texts make in a larger canon of Black girlhood are that girlhood spaces—specifically, friendships, dreams, and desires—represent a different model of existence.

Black Girlhood, Play, and Freedom Dreams

Another component to Black girlhood narratives is the beauty that is realized in expressing dreams, whether in childhood or in adulthood. In the introduction to her most recent collection of short stories, edited and with an introduction by Genevieve West, Mary Helen Washington notes the inclusion of the twenty-one short stories that Hurston wrote between her first short story and the novel. Many of these stories present the locales where Hurston lived and traveled outside of her life in New York City and where she dreamed both of city life and of creating a home.

This idea of dreaming of home is present in Hurston's letters as well, as she writes to her "Godmother" and patron Charlotte Osgood Mason.[1] In one, she is located in New York City (address: 43 West 66th Street) and stated:

> Dear Darling Godmother,
> You have given me the happiest Christmas season of all my life. For the first time ever, I was among friends <u>and</u> well fed and warm. I could give and receive. It was nothing expensive that I had to give, but I could give <u>something</u> as well as receive. I had love. I felt you warm and close and urging me on to happiness. <u>Nothing </u>was lacking, even to the traditional egg-nog.
> Godmother dearest, far-seeing one, you have given me my <u>first</u> Christmas. I mean the first yule season when reality met my dreams. The kind of Christmas that my half-starved child-hood painted.
> Thank you, dear Godmother.
> Zora

Here, Hurston refers to this holiday, where she felt loved and was surrounded by people, as something that she had not received even as a child, with the loss

---

1. Hurston's letters from Moorland-Spingarn Research Center, Howard University.

of her mother and issues with her father and stepmother (verify) leading to her early departure from her home.

The South then becomes a place both for Hurston to dream and of which she dreams. In another letter, she wrote from New York City on Sept. 16, 1932:

> Dear, dear Godmother,
>
> A thousand thanks for the money you sent me. I am very grateful.
>
> I think my concert plans in the South are pretty definite for the fall and winter. I shall not be teaching at all. First of all, Mrs. Bethune was most lovely to me when I went to call on her, but she is having to reduce her faculty instead of adding to it. She said, however, that she would be glad to have me if she can raise a certain amount of money by the time school opens, late in September.
>
> Now, I know that you are wondering what I am doing in New York. Well, the Athenaeum Concert agency in Steinway Hall wired me a ticket to come at once. They saw the concerts last year and want to hook 8 of them this fall. I don't know whether to undertake them or not because I have a very good proposition in the South and feel rather secure there.
>
> Therefore, Godmother darling, it seems that I am about to make a living at last. . . . By the 15th of October I shall be in actual work in Florida and so shall be making money of my own. More than that, I shall have a chance to make a name for myself without the Broadway drawbacks.

Here, Hurston is asking for funds in the letter to continue her lifestyle without the hustle of being located in New York, writing, "If you will, therefore, give me the allowance for October, to allow me to function until my salary begins, I shall be off of your financial hands forever."

Her dreams of being a playwright and making her own money as well are mentioned here and developed in other letters. She writes to Alain Locke from the YWCA (Young Women's Christian Association) of Chicago on October 29, 1934, inviting him there and noting, "My play 'Mule Bone' has been asked for by the Little Theatre in New York, Same director as for 'Run Little Chillun.' I am wondering whether to send it there or to produce it myself here. I have a very good opening. Since all funds for the play and everything else can be had right here, I am wondering if I could not do a better job of interpreting Negro material than any white director ever could." The American South is Hurston's initial site of redreaming and reimagining, but she is continually able to return to that locale and imagine her own future.

New pathways are often the results of dreaming beyond one's world spiritually, physically, emotionally, and psychologically. Morrison's second book, *Sula*, also focuses on dreams that failed to materialize in the Bottom of Medallion, Ohio (named for a trick that a slavemaster played on a slave, telling a slave that the best land was in the "bottom" of Heaven as God looked down). Although *Sula* begins by focusing on the dreams that don't come true in the rocky, hilly soil of the Bottom, we then move through Shadrack's dreams of suicide, and Helene Wright's dreams that fixed her daughter Nel into her own vision of a satisfactory life. Similar to the way Shadrack transforms his death wish into National Suicide Day (a solitary parade of one on January 3 each year), Nel moves from under her mother's fixed hand to imagined visions of a different life after a southern journey to visit her great-grandmother on her deathbed. Morrison wrote:

> [Helene Wright's] daughter was more comfort and purpose than she had ever hoped to find in this life. She rose grandly to the occasion of motherhood—grateful, deep down in her heart, that the child had not inherited the great beauty that was hers: that her skin had dusk in it, that her lashes were substantial but not undignified in their length, that she had taken the broad flat nose of Wiley . . . and his generous lips. (18)

The book continues: "Under Helene's hand the girl became obedient and polite. Any enthusiasms that little Nel showed were calmed by the mother until she drove her daughter's imagination underground" (18).

Helene was a conservative, impressive, regimented woman who "loved her house and enjoyed manipulating her daughter and her husband" (18). She smiles dazzlingly when made to move into the Colored car on a train to see her ailing grandmother, where they would ride for two days. Morrison wrote, "When they changed trains in Birmingham for the last leg of the trip, they discovered what luxury they had been in through Kentucky and Tennessee, where the rest stops had all had colored toilets. After Birmingham there were none" (23). When Helene finally asks another Black woman where she can go, she begins the journey to "yonder" to squat with Nel and the other women in the fields of Meridian, Ellisville, and Hattiesburg, Mississippi, and Slidell, Louisiana, into New Orleans.

The physicality of Black girl bodies is rarely discussed in literature. These bodies are to remain private, whether being celebrated or desecrated. What communication there is, to return to Janie's story, is to be "respectable," to not only keep one's body from others but also keep it also from oneself. Narratives of play rarely include playing with one's own body or body parts. But for Black girls like me, our awareness of our own bodies was always there, as we existed in, and dreamed beyond, the spaces we lived. For Janie, this awareness of her body's sensuality comes initially through nature in her southern childhood home. Dreaming allows the narrator to claim a home wherever she is but also to embrace desires to return home to a physical space as well.

The train that takes Helene to her grandmother, however, does not represent the freedom from matriarchal power that Helene desires but, instead, the freedom for Nel to ultimately relieve herself of the restrictions of social conduct. The two reach Helene's grandmother's house the day after her death, and there, a woman in yellow strikes a match and blows it out to darken her eyebrows: "All the while Helene and Nel watched her. The one in a rage at the folded leaves she had endured, the wooden benches she had slept on, all to miss seeing her grandmother and seeing instead that painted canary . . ." (26). But Nel sees something different after being hugged by Rochelle in a "a quick embrace tighter and harder than one would have imagined her thin soft arms capable of" (27). Nel reflects, "She smelled so nice. And her skin was so soft," to which Helene responds, "Much handled things are always soft" (27). Although neither she nor her mother speaks the language (Creole) that will let them fully understand their environment, Nel imagines that New Orleans, her great-grandmother's house, is freedom itself before that freedom is revoked temporarily by Helene.

Nel dreams, even as her mother tells her to pull her nose (a southern practice to make sure one's nose is long instead of wide), of "the smell and tight, tight hug of the woman in yellow who rubbed burned matches over her eyes" (28). She dreams of her trip, "the urine running down and into her stockings until she learned how to squat properly; the disgust on the face of the dead woman and the sound of the funeral drums" (28):

> She got out of bed and lit the lamp to look in the mirror. There was her face, plain brown eyes, three braids and the nose her mother hated. She looked for a long time and suddenly a shiver ran through her.
>
> "I'm me," she whispered. "Me."
>
> Nel didn't know quite what she meant, but on the other hand she knew exactly what she meant.
>
> "I'm me. I'm not their daughter. I'm not Nel. I'm me. Me."

Every time she said the word me there was a gathering in her like power, like joy, like fear. Back in bed with her discovery, she stared out the window at the dark leaves of the horse chestnut.

"Me," she murmured. And then, sinking deeper into the quilts, "I want . . . I want to be . . . wonderful. Oh, Jesus, make me wonderful." (29)

"Wonderful" represents the beauty of Nel seeing who she is for herself. Nel's dream, before she slept, of the experiences of leaving Medallion then prompted her to:

imagine other trips she would take, alone though, to faraway places. Contemplating them was delicious. Leaving Medallion would be her goal. But that was before she met Sula, the girl she had seen for five years at Garfield Primary but never played with, never knew, because her mother said that Sula's mother was sooty. The trip, perhaps, or her new found me-ness, gave her the strength to cultivate a friend in spite of her mother. (29)

And so, Nel's wishes to move outside of the neatness of her mother's space then led to a place of her own in Sula's.

Sula, the daughter of a "sooty" mother, loves Nel's "oppressively neat" home and sits "still as dawn" on the red velvet sofa (29). Nel, however, prefers Sula's black, "woolly house," which is full of human activity and its detritus, and where Sula's grandmother, Eva, reads dreams (29). Nel, we can argue, finally finds the "excessive" freedom of self-identity, away from her mother's home and through her relationship with Sula. She is able to reconfigure her own limits through her ability to dream, just as Janie's return not to her original home but to the place that she made home becomes beautiful for her. The pathways are not easy and can be dangerous and even treacherous as the girls, then women, search for beautiful spaces of freedom. However, the opportunity to transform one's own circumstances and find their own beauty is worth the risk.

RECESS: for Ruby Bridges, the Little Rock 9, for the little/blk girls, and for Rosa.

Chapter 3

Move

Girlhood and Social Protest

There is a well-known image of Ruby Bridges, dressed and doted for school with a lunchbox in hand as she walks. This image, artfully recreated by Norman Rockwell into his painting *The Problem We All Live With*, painting has only grown more iconic and well cemented into the crux of American art history and the civil rights movement. In a symbolic move, artist Bria Goeller referenced Rockwell's painting in *That Little Girl Was Me*, an adaptation to modern-day politics and the positions of Blacks in modern society: Ruby's shadow is still cast onto the wall; however, this time, it is Vice President (then-Elect) Kamala Harris walking alongside the shadow.

The implication was clear, Harris's ascension to the position of vice president was a landmark moment in civil rights history, and many contemporary political settings and the recreation of *The Problem We All Live With* were both a celebration of the progress since Ruby Bridges's time and a reminder about the prevalent problems that continue to hamper the education of Black students nationwide.

Bridges, herself (who is still alive) has contributed to the more recent literature dedicated to writing about educational desegregation. She authored her own picture book, *Through My Eyes*, telling her famed story as recently as 1991, and, more recently, *This Is Your Time* in 2020, which offers encouragement for the current changemakers challenging individual and institutional racism. Bridges's story is just part of a larger narrative of challenges to equity in the field of education, and other authors have nonfiction and fictional contributions about school integration. Author Ntozake Shange, who is known widely for her choreopoem *for colored girls who have considered suicide/when the rainbow is enuf*, wrote her 1985 novel *Betsey Brown*, which focuses on young Betsey integrating schools in St. Louis, Missouri. Jo Ann Allen Boyce and Debbie Levy published *The Promise of Change: One Girl's Story in the Fight for School Equality* (2019) as a narrative of integrating schools in Clinton, Tennessee, in 1956. These stories stand alongside those of the Little Rock Nine that are based on their experiences in integrating Central High School in Little Rock, Arkansas, in 1957. Their enrollment was followed by what became known as the Little Rock Crisis, when they were prevented from entering the segregated school by then-governor of Arkansas Orval Faubus and resulted in the *Cooper v. Aaron* case of 1958. The narrative of Dorothy Counts (now Scoggins) integrating Harding High School still circulates in Charlotte, North Carolina, as she still speaks out about her experiences that led her parents to withdraw her from Harding during the school year. Yet the return of segregation (or, in some cases, integration that was never truly achieved) does not always receive significant coverage outside of Black communities and narratives.

Ntozake Shange represents the effects of the *Brown v. Board of Education of Topeka* decision in *Betsey Brown*, her 1985 book about a young girl navigating the integration of schools in St. Louis and desiring the safety of her own community. Shange, born in 1948, was a school-age girl in Trenton, New Jersey, at the time the *Brown* decision ended legal racial segregation in public schools. She was six years old at the time of *Brown*, the same age as Ruby Bridges (now Ruby Nell Bridges Hall) was in 1960 when she became widely known as the first African American child to desegregate all-white William Frantz Elementary School in New Orleans on November 14th of that year.

This was three years after the Little Rock Nine, a group of nine African American high school students (both young men and women), enrolled in Little Rock Central High School on September 4, 1957 (www.history.com), followed by the Little Rock Crisis, in which students were initially prevented from entering by Orval Faubus, then-governor of Arkansas.

When we think about Black women's activism in the 1960s and 1970s, these events of the earlier decades would likely have shaped how they were thinking about responses to racism. I argue that texts published during and after the Black Arts movement of the late 1960s—a creative response but also sister to the radical movement—give us a lens into how Black girlhood was witnessed and experienced during the tenuous time of legal desegregation that placed their bodies at the forefront of a public stage.

In *From #BlackLivesMatter to Black Liberation*, Keeanga-Yamahtta Taylor writes, "The aspiration for Black liberation cannot be separated from what happens in the United States as a whole" (193). The command received from each of the authors mentioned in this text is to march, to move forward in whatever way they are able, in the larger contexts of activism. From Ida B. Wells's anti-lynching journalism in the 1890s to the women's suffrage movement, which did not include Black women's right to vote, this chapter also discusses children's roles in movements, from the Children's March in the spring of 1963 in Birmingham, Alabama, to the integration of schools around the South. Where were girls not able to simply play or even just interact with their peers, within and across color lines?

In *Let the Children March* (2018), Monica Clark-Robinson notes the significant dates of 1963, starting with January 14, when Alabama Governor George Wallace called for "segregation now, segregation tomorrow, segregation forever" in his inaugural speech. On April 3, the first organized sit-ins in Birmingham (although not the first in the United States) took place at downtown lunch counters. On April 12, Dr. Martin Luther King Jr. and other protesters are arrested for demonstrating without a permit; and on May 2, the Birmingham Children's Crusade began, in which nine hundred seventy-three young marchers were jailed in a single day; close to one thousand more, mostly under the age of eighteen, were arrested on the following day, a day when Commissioner Theophilus Eugene "Bull" Connor also authorized the use of high-pressure water hoses and police dogs as crowd control. From May 4 to May 9, more adults join the marches and fill the jails that already held thousands of young people to capacity. The agreement that Dr. King and other protest organizers reached with city leaders to begin the process of desegregation began on May 10, and that date also marked a rally of the Ku Klux Klan and the bombing of the home of Alfred Daniel Williams "A. D." King, Dr. King's brother. On May 19, 1963, the school board expelled many of the student demonstrators, but those expulsions were overturned three days later.

Clark-Robinson's narrative is just one of many in which the activism of young people is displayed along with that of adults. In *A Taste of Power*, Elaine Brown writes about having to walk to school, go by neighbors' houses for food, and stealing bread, but her mother, a strong woman with "beautiful hair" (22)—sent her to a nursery school operated by charity agency. Brown writes, "they made girls' dresses where she worked and she would press some and also steal some for me, so I would always look pretty" (22). She describes watching her mother work and adds a narrative of her grandmother and her belief in Jesus. Brown's mother thought that she was "too precious for public schools" and signed her up for an "exceptional" school. She writes: "There was a four-year waiting list for the special school. My mother determined, however, that I would go there right away; there would be no waiting list for me. . . . Nearly every day, she would call every colored professional she knew of, including our neighborhood doctor, the funeral home director, and the minister at Jones Tabernacle A.M.E. Church" (24). As a result of her mother's diligence, she was enrolled.

Although calling around for school enrollment is not explicitly political, Brown's mother was determined not to let class hold her daughter in an inferior place. She challenged the politics of the unspoken rules of racial and social hierarchies that said that Brown did not belong. At this school, Brown was a regular kid who liked class, songs, and games (24), but she also sought to be part of this group in an intentional way: "I did anything to belong among them, those white children and white teachers," (30) as she tried to leave her home on York Street behind.

Brown's shifting between worlds to be included looked differently, as she writes that she had to become something else to fit in: "Finally, I became white. At least until 2:17 pm, when school was let out, when the bell would toll and the curtain falls and I would be returned by fate through the subway tunnel, down Susquehanna, down 21st Street or 2051 West York Street, and back to being black" (31). She then repeats the adage, "If you black, git back" (31). Determining where to belong became her plight, and Brown had to decide what she was and was not as well. She notes:

> I did not want to get back . . . I was really not like the other colored girls. My mother had told me that. White people were telling me that. I did not belong on York Street. I belonged in their world. I had not only learned to talk white and act white I could do white things. (31)

The "white things" included classical music, piano, and theater, with religion replacing them later: "Replacing Chopin, the ballet, the theater, and Thaddeus Stevens was Bible School" (33). But after these requirements, there were songs and games, double dutch, and clapping games (34–35). For Brown, who would go on to hold a primary role as Black Panther Party chairwoman, prison activist, writer, and even singer, learning to exist in the world came from her mother first determining for her that she was different, although her model of moving through the world challenged her own identity.

> I believe in living./I believe in the spectrum/of Beta days and Gamma people./I believe in sunshine./In windmills and waterfalls,/tricycles and rocking chairs./And i believe that seeds grow into sprouts./And sprouts grow into trees. I believe in the magic of the hands./And in the wisdom of the eyes./I believe in rain and tears./And in the blood of infinity. (Assata Shakur, 2)

Another example of marching or moving forth through narrative came from Assata Shakur, who was shot and taken on the New Jersey Turnpike on May 2, 1973, after attempts to "criminalize, defame, harass and intimidate Assata" from at least 1971 (viii). Angela Davis's foreword to *Assata: An Autobiography* reads, "On May 2, 1973, when the shooting on the New Jersey Turnpike occurred, Assata was 'wanted' for all these crimes. The irony is that not one of the charges led to conviction. When she was apprehended, shot down on the New Jersey Turnpike, leading to her only conviction, she should have enjoyed the presumption of innocence that the Fifth Amendment to the U.S. Constitution is supposed to grant to any of us when accused" (ix). Davis continues that Shakur was stopped by New Jersey State Trooper James Harper as she traveled on the New Jersey Turnpike "for reasons consistent with the FBI COINTELPRO guidelines, which directed that activists be arrested for minor traffic violations. The Pontiac allegedly had defective taillights. Harper's testimony, however, leaves open the suggestion that the Pontiac was simply a target" (ix). On the basis of her own legal experience, Davis summarizes Shakur's treatment as such:

> In the history of New Jersey, no woman pretrial detainee or prisoner has ever been treated as she was, continuously confined in a men's prison, under twenty-four-hour surveillance of her most intellectual sustenance, adequate medical attention, and exercise, and without the company of other women for all the years she was in their custody. . . . As you read her story, imagine the effect these conditions must have had on this proud and sensitive woman. (x)

Much of what we know about Shakur's story is not in her own words, but as Davis, who is also part of her legacy of activism, explains, we have to read her story to know her experience and the impact of state politics and violence on her body. Davis narrates:

> The jury at Assata's trial for the same offenses was permitted to speculate that her "mere presence" at the scene of violence, with weapons in the vehicle, was sufficient to sustain a conviction—even though three neurologists testified at the trial that her median nerve had been severed by gunshot wounds, rendering her unable to pull a trigger, and that her clavicle had been shattered by a shot that could only have been made while she was seated in the car with her hands raised. Other experts testified that the neutron activation analysis administered by the police right after

the shootout showed no gun residue on her fingers, meaning she had not shot a weapon. She was also convicted of possession of weapons—none of which could be identified as having been handled by her—and of the attempted murder of state trooper Harper, who had sustained a minor injury at the shootout. (xi)

Assata Shakur's narrative, in her own words, challenges the image that the media tried to paint of her as a violent woman. From her own story, we see her narrative of growing up in Wilmington, North Carolina, with her grandparents through the mothering and separation of her own daughter.

Shakur writes: "We moved into a big wooden house on Seventh Street in Wilmington, North Carolina. It was the house my grandfather had grown up in. It had a wraparound porch with a big green swing and, of course, rosebushes in the front yard and a pecan tree in the back" (19). Finding the truth behind the house—she states that her grandparents were forced to buy the house after thinking it belonged to her great-grandfather Pappa Linc (he had only been given use of house for his lifetime)—does not deter her from being full of pride at what her family owns and is able to do.

> *"Who's better than you?"*
> *"Nobody."*
> *"Who?"*
> *"Nobody."*
> *"Get that head up."*
> *"Yes."*
> *"Yes, who?"*
> *"Yes, Grandmommy."*
> *"I want that head held up high, and i don't want you taking no mess from anybody, you understand?"*
> *"Yes, Grandmommy."*
> *"Don't you let me hear about anybody walking over my grandbaby."*
> *"No, Grandmommy."*
> *"I don't want nobody taking advantage of you, you hear me?"* (19)

Shakur writes: "All of my family tried to instill in me a sense of personal dignity, but my grandmother and my grandfather were really fanatic about it. Over and over they would tell me, 'You're as good as anyone else. Don't let anybody tell you that they're better than you.' My grandparents strictly forbade me to say 'yes ma'am' and 'yes sir' or to look down at my shoes or to make subservient gestures when talking to white people. 'You look them in the eye when you talk to them,' i was told. 'And speak up like you've got some sense.' I was told to speak in a loud, clear voice and to hold my head up high, or risk having my grandparents knock it off my shoulders" (19). She was to respect adults who respected her and her family and not to think herself inferior to those who did not.

> I was to be polite and respectful to adults, to say "good morning" or "good evening" as i passed the neighbors' houses. Any kind of back talk or sass was simply out of the question. My grandparents didn't even permit me to answer questions with a simple "yes" or "no." Instead I had to say "yes, Grandmother" or "no, Grandfather." But when it came to dealing with white people in the segregated South, my grandmother would tell me, menacingly, "Don't you respect nobody that don't respect you, you hear me?" "Yes, Grandmother," i would answer, my voice almost a whisper. "Speak up!" she would tell me repeatedly, something she seemed hell-bent on making me do. (19)

Shakur's grandmother would not allow her to come home with inferior goods from the store, and if she did, she would have to return for an exchange or refund. "If the store owner sold me something that my grandmother didn't like, i would have to return to the store and get the thing changed or get my money back. 'You speak up loud and clear. Don't let me have to go down to that store.' Scared to death of the fuss my grandmother would make if she had to go to the store herself, i would hurry back to the store, prepared to raise almighty hell.'" (20). She was taught not to be mistreated and to "take no mess off nobody":

> "Don't you let anybody mistreat you, you hear? We're not raising you up to be mistreated, you hear? I don't want you taking no mess off of nobody, you understand?" "Yes, Grandmother," i would answer, for what seemed like the millionth time, wondering why my grandmother liked to repeat herself so often. The tactics that my grandparents used were crude, and i hated it when they would repeat everything so often. But the lessons they taught me, more than anything else i learned in life, helped me to deal with the things i would face growing up in amerika. (20)

As in Brown's later narrative, Shakur's grandparents still compared things to white America. "For them, being 'just as good' as white people meant having what white people had. They would tell me to go to school and study so that i could have a nice house and nice clothes and a nice car. 'White people don't want to see us with nothing,' they would tell me. 'That's why you've got to get your education so that you can be somebody and have something in your life.'" (20). They were concerned with her being "somebody" important. But for Shakur, she just wanted to feel joy. She writes: "Becoming 'somebody' in life just didn't mean too much to me. I wanted to feel happy, to feel good" (20).

Like other Black girl coming-of-age narratives, Shakur had to think of herself as being in conversation with those who came before her:

> My awareness of class differences in the Black community came at an early age. Although my grandmother taught me more about being proud and strong than anyone i know, she had a lot of Booker T. Washington, pull yourself up by the bootstraps, "talented tenth" ideas. She had worked hard and had made a decent living as a pieceworker in a factory, but she had other ideas for me. She was determined that i would become part of Wilmington's talented tenth—the privileged class—part of the so-called Black bourgeoisie. (21)

As the daughter of divorced parents, Shakur lived with her mother, aunt, and grandparents in Jamaica, New York, until she was three, when her grandparents sold the house and moved "down South," and she moved with them (18). These are the years that stay with her throughout the narrative. Assata also thinks of her time in the South as she is being examined by medics:

> Time passed. I was floating off again. It felt so weird, like a dream, a nightmare. More time passed. It seemed like forever. I was in and out, in and out. . . A rough voice asked, 'Is she dead yet?' I floated off again. . . . The bubbles in my chest felt like they were growing bigger. When they burst, my whole chest shattered. I faded again and it was down South in the summertime. I thought about my grandmother. (4)

"I was born"

Assata Shakur's narrative also connects to the "I was born" beginnings of narratives of enslavement in the nineteenth century. Those used birth as a statement of something evident (existence) but also unfathomable (humanity). Shakur begins the third chapter with this questioning of her entrance into the world. She writes: "The FBI cannot find any evidence that i was born. On my FBI Wanted poster, they list my birth date as July 16, 1947, and in parentheses, 'not substantiated by birth records'" and continues, "Anyway, i was born" in a statement of the obvious but that requests, that requires, additional information (18).

Shakur's telling of her own story also contains her birth name, JoAnne Deborah Byron, her birth order as an older sister, and confirmation of her brilliance but also her ambivalent personality. "I am told that i was a fat, happy baby and that i was talking in complete sentences when i was about nine months old. They say that i was lazy, though, that i talked way before i learned to walk. Everybody says that i had my days mixed up with my nights and kept everybody up at all night" (18).

Her narrative of her grandmother was to be forbidden to play with "alley rats" when she had no idea what they were:

> I received strict orders to abandon my penchant for alley rats and play with "decent children." But we could never agree on who "decent children" were. Decent children, to my grandmother, were a whole 'nother story. "Decent children" came from "decent families." How did you know what a decent family was? A decent family lived in a decent house. How did you know what a decent house was? A decent house was fixed up nice and had a sidewalk in front of it. Decent families didn't let their kids play in the street with no shoes on and didn't let their kids say "ain't." Little did my grandmother know that *ain't* was my favorite word once i got two feet out of her hearing range. My grandmother had a little alley rat right under her roof and she didn't even know it. (21)

The decent children, Shakur writes, were the offspring of Wilmington's Black doctors, lawyers, preachers, and undertakers; schoolteachers, barbershop owners, and the editor of the "colored" newspaper were also decent, but she adds, "My grandmother would have caught a shitfit if she had known that one of her favorite little decent kids' favorite game was playing show and tell with his ding-a-ling and threatening to pee on everybody" (21–22). The politics of respectability were in full effect, as Shakur refused to adopt the same thoughts about her friends as her elder: "My grandmother and i waged a standoff battle damn near until i was grown. It wasn't that i wanted to defy her, it was that i just liked who i liked. I didn't care what kind of house my friends had or whether or not they lived in alleys. All that mattered was whether i liked them. I was convinced then, and i'm still convinced, that in some things kids have a lot more sense than adults" (22).

Lessons she learned from her grandmother and her family included the value of working for themselves, as they lived close to Carolina Beach, North

Carolina, outside of Wilmington (with its own stories of resistance going back to the 1898 incidents in which Black Power and positions were challenged) and owned their own land and stores.

> Their last name was Freeman, and they were famous for being high-strung, quick-tempered, and emotional. They seldom worked for anybody, choosing instead to live on the land their father had left them. They worked as farmers and fishermen, and they owned small stores. . . . My grandmother's father was a Cherokee Indian. He died when my grandmother was very young. Nobody knows too much about him, except that, somehow, he acquired a great deal of land and left it to his children. The land was very valuable because much of it bordered either on the river or on the ocean. Everybody had a different theory about what my great-grandfather had done to acquire it. But it was because of this land that my grandparents had moved down South. (23)

Like many other Black families, a return to the land was what brought them there but also what reminded them of the reasons their ancestors had left. She writes:

> In 1950, the year we moved to Wilmington, the South was completely segregated. Black people were forbidden to go many places, and that included the beach. Sometimes they would travel all the way to South Carolina just to see the ocean. My grandparents decided to open a business on their land. It consisted of a restaurant, lockers where people could change their clothes, and an area for dancing and hanging out. (23)

Before one of her own resistance, Shakur's story is one of her grandparents' refusal to remain in the boxes assigned by society and also one of their entrepreneurship as they committed to providing for their own people. It is through their entrepreneurial activism that she finds the narrative of her family and of her people:

> The popular name for the beach was Bop City, although my grandparents insisted on calling it Freeman's beach. Throughout my childhood, the name Freeman had no particular significance. It was a name just like any other name. It wasn't until i was grown and began to read Black history that i discovered the significance of the name. After slavery, many Black people refused to use the last name of their masters. They called themselves "Freeman" instead. The name was also used by Africans who were

freed before slavery was "officially" abolished, but it was mainly after the abolition of chattel slavery that many Black people changed their names to Freeman. After learning this, i saw my ancestors in a new light (23).

Shakur's family's narrative also became her own, including working in the store, selling small items, and collecting fifty cents for parking "Because there was no road to our beach (the paved road ended with the white section), [and] my grandparents had to pay for a dirt road and parking lot to be laid over the sand . . ." (24). They were visited by real ghosts, "phantoms of the parking lot" who were unhappy with their success and caused her grandfather to put a large chain across the entrance to the parking lot, which eliminated the "nightly visitors" (27). Shakur also tells the story of her grandmother's refusal to let a white man turn around in their parking lot, asserting her own control of their property (27).

Her grandparents were not always able to control the narrative of racism. She tells the story of not knowing that they were not allowed in the zoo.

> every day i would beg, plead, whine, and nag my grandmother to take me to the zoo. It was almost an obsession. She would always say that "one day" she would take me, but "one day" never came. I would sit in the car pouting, thinking how mean she was. I thought that she had to be the meanest woman on the face of the earth. Finally, with the strangest look on her face, she told me that we were not allowed in the zoo. Because we were Black. (27)

Black people were also not permitted to go into the amusement park at Carolina Beach. In a scene reminiscent of Frederick Douglass's musing of the free boats at sea in Maryland, Shakur writes of a deprivation of her own freedom.

> Every time we passed it i looked at the merry-go-round and the Ferris wheel and the little cars and airplanes and my heart would just long to ride them. But my favorite forbidden ride had little boats in a pool of water, and every time i passed them i felt frustrated and deprived. Of course, persistent creature that i am, i always asked to be taken on the rides, knowing full well what the answer would be. (28)

Finally, Shakur's mother, in her own spirit of resistance, pretends not to speak English to get tickets on a ride. She writes: "I couldn't believe it. All at once we were laughing and giggling and riding the rides. All the white people were staring at us, but we didn't care. We were busy having a ball. When i got into one of those little boats, my mother practically had to drag me out. I was in my glory. When we finished the rides we went to the Dairy Queen for ice cream. We sang and laughed all the way home." She continues:

> When we got home my mother explained that she had been speaking Spanish and had told the managers that she was from a Spanish country and that if he didn't let us in she would call the embassy and the United Nations and i don't know who all else. We laughed and talked about it for days. But it was a lesson i never forgot. Anybody, no matter who they were, could come right off the boat and get more rights and respect than amerikan-born Blacks. (28)

Before even going to school in Wilmington, a nursery school for Black people but where [she] "learned the fundamentals of reading, writing, and arithmetic" at four years old, Shakur was prepared for the world beyond segregated spaces. She spent most of first grade in New York with her mother and the rest of first grade and all of second grade back down South.

> Of course, our school was segregated, but the teachers took more of an interest in our lives because they lived in our world, in the same neighborhoods. They knew what we were up against and what we would be facing as adults, and they tried to protect us as much as they could. More than once we were punished because some children had made fun of a student who was poor and badly dressed. I'm not saying that segregation was a good system. Our schools were inferior. The books were used and torn, handed down from white schools. We received only a fraction of the state money allotted to white schools, and the conditions under which many Black children received an education can only be described as horrible. But Black children encountered support and understanding and encouragement instead of the hostile indifference they often met in the "integrated" schools. (28–29)

Here, Shakur describes the knowledge and acknowledgment of inferior schools but also the tools of resistance in the forms of "support . . . understanding, and encouragement" to help them challenge the assertion of white mainstream society that they were, in any way, "less than" because of the resources that were withheld from them.

Shakur's story of resistance continues well beyond her nursery and elementary school days, but, just as for Brown, Davis, and others, it is important to assert that she was acculturated by her family as a child into a spirit of acknowledging but refusing to accept implicit or blatant racism that came through systems of education and even through play. This refusal would later carry her into the survival of the fight for her life.

After moving through integrated schools in New York and beginning her career, after surviving the acquittal of several charges but still held captive by others, Assata Shakur went to Cuba and spent five years without talking to her family. As with her own narrative, she has to prove that her daughter was born.

> In order for Kakuya to get her passport, she needed a birth certificate. My mother told me that for ten years Elmhurst Hospital had refused to issue Kakuya a birth certificate. Finally, after months of hassling, [her aunt] Evelyn had to go to kourt to get a document proving that my daughter had been born. (273)

In Cuba, she and her family found a place of freedom that they could not find before, as she writes: "We were here together in their land, my small little family, holding each other after so long. There was no doubt about it, our people would one day be free. The cowboys and bandits didn't own the world" (274). Passing the torch throughout her family, Assata Shakur is both light and legacy for those who opt out of the systems whose only purpose is to oppress. This activism is continued in fiction and nonfiction, in Angie Thomas's *The Hate U Give*, Charlene Carruthers's *Unapologetic*, Patrisse Cullors's *When They Call You a Terrorist*, and numerous other texts.

Connecting past and present characters around what dreaming allows for Black girls, this chapter also discusses the aesthetics of Black girlhood in poetry such as Jacqueline Woodson's *Brown Girl Dreaming* to narrate the experiences of civil rights struggles in the South (e.g., Greenville, South Carolina, where Woodson's grandparents lived) and moments of poetic liberation through play. In a lecture titled "Radical Love and Liberation" (on December 5, 2020), author adrienne maree brown asks, "What are the original instructions that [we're] supposed to move through in this world?" I add here: What instructions do we give others? What are the typologies through which we interpret Black girlhood?

These narratives were revisited in Ntozake Shange's account of 1955 "not being a good year for little/blk girls" in *for colored girls who have considered suicide/when the rainbow is enuf*, performed and published in 1976 (and referring to integration movements but also connected to the murder of Emmett Till and the Montgomery bus boycotts, and the impact of all of these on Black girls).

Teaching [to] the State

Histories show us that Black children, including Black girls, have long been at the center of discussion on policy and how in 1954, the *Brown v. Board of Education of Topeka* decision was passed, which stated that segregation in schools was not, indeed, equal and resulted in the change of status, if not the treatment, of Black children as members of an integrated populace with the promise of equal rights. We know from images of turmoil in this integration—the National Guard at the site of Central High School in Little Rock, Arkansas; the discussion of discomfort and maltreatment in *The Promise of Change* by Jo Ann Allen Boyce, which poetically details the author's narrative of integrating schools in Clinton, Tennessee; and other narratives—that inclusion was neither guaranteed nor accepted.

How are Black girlhood narratives creating and curating narratives of education? Revisiting the focus on "social graces" in Charlotte Hawkins Brown's *The Correct Thing to Do, to Say, to Wear* (1940), as Brown founded and led the Palmer Memorial Institute in Gibsonville, North Carolina (east of Greensboro), in 1902 for fifty years, leads to a discussion of attention to the educational system as something that both opens up space for and limits Black girls. Brown was born in Henderson, North Carolina, in 1883 to descendants of enslaved people and moved with her family in 1888 to Cambridge, Massachusetts, near Boston, for "better social, economic, and educational opportunities." She was mentored by Alice Freeman Palmer, an educator who helped to sponsor her schooling, and returned to North Carolina after a year of junior college to teach rural Black students through a job sponsored by the American Missionary Association.

Brown came to Bethany Institute in Sedalia, North Carolina, in 1901, and although she began repairing the rundown school, the American Missionary Association decided to close it. The eighteen-year-old Brown sought funding from her friends in the North, moved the school to a blacksmith's shed across the street, and built a new campus with over two hundred acres and two new buildings. All of the trustees were African American, and Palmer Institute offered college preparatory classes in junior and senior high school. Describing the Palmer Institute, the website North Carolina Historic Sites (historicsites .nc.gov) notes, "Students were divided into small circle groups with teachers who served as counselors and advisers. Each student received personal training in character development and appearance. Additionally, all students had to work one hour per day for the school as service learning." Even after two buildings caught on fire, Brown maintained significant funding for the school, especially from white Northerners, for the purpose of educating Black Americans beyond traditional training. The website states, "Brown introduced more liberal arts classes and advanced math and science courses for Palmer students. They even studied African American history at a time when no other North Carolina school was teaching it" (historicsites.nc.gov).

During a year traveling in Europe, Brown had the opportunity to travel and study with Black educators Mary McLeod Bethune and Nannie Helen Burroughs, and they were known all together as the "Three Bs of Education." The site states: "The Three Bs believed in combining a holistic triangle of ideas and lessons to achieve racial equality: Brown's triangle combined education, religion, and deeds; Bethune's triangle was 'the head, the heart, and the hand'; Burroughs's was 'the book, the Bible, and the broom'" and continues that Brown became a nationally known speaker by the mid-1920s who emphasized teaching these concepts through culture and liberal arts to promote racial uplift.

Brown also started the first school for "delinquent" African American girls, a junior college, and a new boys' dormitory; and, in 1937, she closed the elementary and junior college departments and convinced Guilford County officials to open the county's first public rural high school for African American students. Her efforts and writing earned her national acclaim; she became known as the "first lady of social graces" and was featured in *Ebony* magazine after raising one hundred thousand dollars for an endowment for Palmer, then known as "the only . . . school of its kind in America." Palmer became and is now a state historic site and was the first state-supported site to honor contributions of African Americans and women.

Other memorials to African American women in education are not as prominent, but their stories still exist. Although we focus on Rosa Parks's incredible efforts that sparked the Montgomery bus boycott of 1955–56, Claudette Colvin's story in March 1955 is also dynamic. In *Claudette Colvin: Twice Toward Justice*, Phillip Hoose writes: "On Monday, May 17, 1954, in the case of *Brown v. Board of Education of Topeka*, the U.S. Supreme Court outlawed racial segregation in public schools. It was a solid punch to Jim Crow, one that produced powerful shock waves throughout the South" (9). He continues:

> The ruling allowed black students to anticipate a different future and emboldened a few of them to try to make it happen. One such student was fifteen-year-old Claudette Colvin, whose school had been studying black

history almost nonstop for a solid month. Around 3:30 on March 2, 1955, this slim, bespectacled high school junior boarded the Highland Gardens bus with a few of her friends and slid into a window seat on the left side, behind the white section. She piled her textbooks on her lap, smoothed her blue dress, and settled back for a five-block ride that not only would change the course of her life but would spark the most important social movement in U.S. history. (9)

The book details Colvin's narrative of being a fifteen-year-old student who had a knowledge of Black history, learned at school. It discusses her sitting behind the white section, being asked to move, and not doing so. But it also discusses her childhood in Pine Level, Alabama, before getting to this moment.

Chapter two, "Coot," notes: "Pine Level didn't have much more than a few shacks for the sharecropper families, a schoolhouse, a church, and a general store, but I was at home in all of it. I floated free, and slept at the homes of my mom's friends as much as in my own bed. They all raised me together" (12). It continues: "Other nights I slept at Mama Sweetie's, a tiny woman in her sixties who was the best reader in Pine Level. She had read the entire Bible many times. She had her own blue-covered Webster's dictionary. Mama Sweetie taught practically every child in Pine Level their ABCs and how to write their names and how to count to a hundred, using peanuts" (14). The narrative adds that the school was "a one-room white wooden building with red trim," with a potbellied stove in the middle and a picture of Abraham Lincoln on the wall. "One teacher taught all six elementary grades, and sat us in sections around the room, grade by grade, two to a desk. The room was rarely full because students kept getting pulled away to do farmwork . . ." (14).

Hoose cites Colvin's love of school as she came to consciousness of her education:

I memorized the Dick and Jane reader so my teacher would think I could already read. One day she asked me to read aloud, but I got way out ahead of the text. She couldn't figure out what was going on. . . . I learned the entire second grade in advance just by listening to Annie—she was a year older than me—and by hearing Mama Sweetie read from her Bible and her Webster's dictionary. When it came time for me to start second grade I could already read and write and spell and even do some arithmetic. They tested me and told me to go sit with the third graders. After that, I was always younger than the other kids in my class. (14)

This is not the narrative we hear of Claudette Colvin, who is still very much alive in 2021. The story continues that she could not become the face of the civil rights movement, although she also refused to move from her bus seat because, at fifteen, she was pregnant. Although her narrative shows her love for education and the stories that sparked her resistance, it also becomes one of not "fitting" the model of a poster child for the desegregation movement.

Other stories of desegregation and integration have become part of popular culture, including Jo Ann Allen Boyce's *This Promise of Change: One Girl's Story in the Fight for School Equality*, written with Debbie Levy. The background of *This Promise* states that "Despite the Constitution's 'equal protection' guarantee, the U.S. Supreme Court found no constitutional defect in segregation. To the contrary, in 1896, in the case of *Plessy v. Ferguson,* the Court said that facilities that were racially 'separate' could be considered 'equal'—or at least equal enough'" (1) and continues:

> In 1954 came *Brown v. Board of Education*. In that case, the Supreme Court reversed the position it had held in a line of cases since *Plessy*. Those old decisions were wrong, the justices ruled. "Separate but equal" schools were *not* equal. They were not equal even if the buildings, supplies, books, and facilities of schools for black children were brought up to par with schools for whites. Racially segregated schools deprived African American children of equal educational opportunities and were unconstitutional—period. (1–2)

As is evident across states and school systems, many school boards and systems made no effort to comply. Levy adds that, "Some states passed laws to punish people who attempted to comply with *Brown v. Board*. Some made plans to shut down their public school systems rather than allow black and white children to go to school together," concluding that, "If *Brown v. Board's* promise of change was to become reality, people had to take action" (2).

Boyce's story, written in poetry, illustrates the literal promise of change that many Black families took on to educate their children. Her story takes place in Clinton, Tennessee, miles from Knoxville, where Black children had to travel to attend school. Boyce describes "Clinton, Tennessee, Our Town" as "up on the Hill . . . a friendly fine town" (8) and describes "Clinton, Tennessee, Their Town" as "friendly and fine too—/with white people friendly and fine/to each other as they go about/the business of running the town" and as "and friendly and fine/to black people who stay in our places./And we do stay in our places,/which is always/a place where we know/friendly white smiles/

can turn upside down/in a quick minute/if we try to move these lines/between white and black" (9).

Boyce knew "something about their town," because her mother worked for a white family, cooking and keeping house with a library "right at home" for the Crenshaws. Her mother brought home books that the Crenshaws were finished with. Boyce continues: "My favorite ever is *The Robe,*/a story that shows just how much/Jesus has to put up with,/and just how strong/ Jesus had to be/to go through what He went through,/and yet still He said:/ Love thy neighbor," (11) adding, "If my house were overflowing with books,/ and I needed to make room/for more books, or clothes, or furniture,/I would find a book other than/ *The Robe* to give up,/but if Mrs. Crenshaw had to part with it,/I'm glad it found its way to me" (11). Tongue-in-cheek in reference to what the Crenshaw family should have kept for themselves, she refers to the religious mission taken on by some white families that actually had the reverse effect of encouraging her.

Boyce characterizes the segregation narrative for Black families in Clinton, where a sign reads "Welcome to Clinton, 'A Wonderful Place to Live'" (16).

"Clinton: Our Town" reads: "3,500 white people/+/220 black people/+/1 movie theater, where Negroes may only sit in the balcony/+/1 swimming pool, where Negroes may not go at all/+/1 fun rec center, with bowling alleys, ping-pong tables,/badminton—but not for Negroes/+/1 public library (only, Negroes aren't part of the "public")/+/1 public high school (whites only) (13). . . . "*Segregation.*/Separate, not equal./Segregation. The way it is and always has been." (14)

She continues that, on the "good side of things," they have two of their own churches as opposed to the "gym at the Negro elementary school,/where all us kids hang out" but muses,

"We don't need white people/to be our friends./We like the friends we have, thank you very much!" (15). She also describes the white family across the street, called "white trash" by other whites in town for interacting with Black families, stating, "I call this neighborly, not trashy" (15).

However, Boyce also cites the feeling of being a child and having full knowledge that life is not equal: "The worst for me, I'd say,/is the feeling I get at Hoskins Drugstore,/where my friends and I go/after the school bus drops us off/at the end of the long ride back/from where we go to high school/at the Negro high school/clear over in Knoxville./The feeling is that I better hurry up,/buy my candy bar and get out,/because they want our money/but don't really want us as customers," concluding that "the candy isn't as sweet as it was/when I was younger/and didn't notice the bitter taste" (16).

Boyce looks to a day in the future in "One Day, Too," when freedom will truly exist for Black families. "We all have a father, an uncle, a brother/ who does yard work or handyman work/for a white family,/and we all see/ what it would be like to be more free/in where we go, how we speak, what we can do./. I would like that, one day, too." (12). In "Keep Your Head Up," she adds, "When I taste the bitter,/when I feel the pain,/from the daily slights/ like a spreading stain. . . . 'You're good as anyone'—the words my parents say. 'God has made us equal./Our prayers show me the way.' Grandmother's always told me/'You keep your head up high'—/These words,/those thoughts,/ this faith—/They lift me up./I fly" (17–18). Boyce's narrative of what it takes "to fly" provides additional context to the visual images that circulate with angry white mobs surrounding one or only a few African American students. One that resonates in particular is the World Press Photo of the year in 1957, of Dorothy Counts (now Scoggins), who integrated Harding High School in Charlotte, North Carolina, before her parents moved her north to Philadelphia to attend school while living with her aunt and uncle, because of the ways she was verbally and physically abused at Harding (including being spat on and having erasers thrown at her head). Counts-Scoggins' parents withdrew her from Harding when the police chief told them he could not guarantee her protection.

Her father made this statement: "It is with compassion for our native land and our love for our daughter Dorothy that we withdraw her as a student at Harding High School. As long as we felt she could be protected from bodily injury and insults within the school's walls and upon the school premises, we were willing to grant her desire to study at Harding." After sophomore year at an integrated public school in Yeadon, Counts-Scoggins was homesick and returned to North Carolina to attend the private all-girls Allen School, where she graduated and then returned to Charlotte to attend historically Black Johnson C. Smith University, where she graduated with a degree in psychology in 1964. She continues to work with children from underserved families and communities and to advocate for the stories of Charlotte and for the Beatties Ford Road corridor of Charlotte to be preserved.

Boyce also narrates her schooling experiences in detail, as she writes about Green McAdoo Grammar School, previously called Clinton Colored School, which was only for Negro students and renamed after a Buffalo Soldier. In

"Things I Know," she writes: "Before Clinton Colored School, the Freed-men's Bureau had built a school on the same site also for Negroes only "and the white folks burned it down/out of hate./But then it was rebuilt/and the rebuilding was led by two men—/one who used to own slaves,/and the other who used to be a slave . . . isn't history strange?" (21).

This "strange history" includes "Two little classrooms for eight grades of children/outdated books cast off from the whites-only school,/old desks carved so deeply with someone else's initials/that your pencil pokes through your paper/into the canyon of that carving—none of this is good enough" (21) but also knows that she "loved that itty-bitty/not real pretty/school up on the Hill" (22). After grammar school, the options decrease for Black students: "Ninth grade:/not in Clinton,/not if you're a black kid./Negroes want more education?/Leave town" (22). Those who want to continue education have to ride the bumpy bus along twisty roads to Knoxville: "Separate./Segregated./ That's why we were sent here/If *race* should make me feel at home./it failed" (23). Austin High School in tenth grade shifts her perspective: "New school,/ same bumpy roads,/but no more tears for me./I'm stronger than I was before:/ I'll live." And concludes, "I live./I give it time./I give this place a chance./ Big-city school and small-town girl/make friends" (23). Friendship becomes the salve for enduring the resistance to providing a solid education for African Americans in town until equal opportunities are available.

Constructing a Sense of Self

I return to radically creative responses that helped communities, even today, understand the significance of movement for Black girls in the context in which they existed. Even in the later memoirs *Assata: An Autobiography*, by Assata Shakur, and *Taste of Power*, by Elaine Brown, these activists return to their stages of girlhood to think about who they were and who taught them to stand in the strength of their identities. I am interested in how they came to see themselves as activists and what lessons they learned, and what we can learn, from Black girlhood activism.

The Black Woman, by Toni Cade (who became Toni Cade Bambara), became one of the first stories, if not the first, about the experiences of Black women in narrative, memoir, and essay around political and social issues as well as ideas around identity, beauty, and nationalism. It also marked much of the emotional and physical labor exerted during the Black Power and Black Arts movements to advance not only the rights of African Americans but of women specifically. However, Black women's activism, as we know it, did not start during the Black Power movement or the late 1960s, or even during the preceding and overlapping civil rights era.

When Cade dictates "a turning toward each other" (7) in the preface of *The Black Woman*, she argues for the communal practice, specifically among Black women, as the salve from the harm that they endure in larger society. However, if Black women are experiencing these "exploitive and dehumanizing systems," including the impact of "'mainstream' culture that restricts them from outside and within," so, I argue, are Black girls. Yet, in the systematic representations that we usually see of them (counted as numbers and statistics, perhaps, but without having their stories highlighted), it is not until Black women's writing turns to Black girlhood that they are truly represented.

Cade continues: "Our art, protest, dialogue no longer spring from the impulse to entertain, or to indulge or enlighten the conscience of the enemy; white people, whiteness, or racism; men, maleness, or chauvinism: America or imperialism . . . depending on your viewpoint and your terror. Our energies now seem to be invested and are in turn derived from a determination to touch and to unify. What typifies the current spirit is an embrace, an embrace of the community and a hardheaded attempt to get basic with each other" (7). The turn to each other that she highlights—through groups, discussion clubs, cooperative businesses, nurseries, caucuses and educational opportunities (9), in addition to publications—also means a *re*-turn to the ways in which Black women thought about ourselves from very early stages of existence to figure out what we need.

Poet and writer Nikki Giovanni began her career thinking about Black empowerment through *Black Feeling, Black Talk/Black Judgement* (1970) but continued into narratives of empowerment for children, such as *Spin A Soft Black Song* (1987) and her even more recent picture book *Rosa*, for which she took a trip to Selma and Montgomery, Alabama, in 2004 for research purposes. Although Rosa Parks' story is widely known, Giovanni adds the community of Black women who supported her to the story of Parks's resistance to moving on a bus for white patrons.

Giovanni writes, "Rosa saw that the section reserved for blacks was full, but she noticed the neutral section, the part of the bus where blacks or whites could sit, had free seats. The left side of the aisle had two seats and on the right side a man was sitting next to the window. Rosa decided to sit next to him. She did not remember his name, but she knew his face. His son, Jimmy, came frequently to the NAACP Youth Council affairs. . . ." Here, she positions

Parks's activism within the context of community through the Youth Council (for which she was the secretary) and familiarity with community. She also reminds the reader of a woman's designated place, even in spaces of mobility. "Rosa settled her sewing bag and her purse near her knees, trying not to crowd Jimmy's father. Men take up more space, she was thinking as she tried to squish her packages closer. The bus made several more stops, and the two seats opposite her were filled by blacks. She sat on her side of the aisle daydreaming about her good day and planning her special meal for her husband." Even on her own time, Parks's narrative is tied to moving from paid labor to domestic work for her husband's and the family's meal. This is an illustration of a "woman's work," even as it is desired to please in partnership.

As the illustration by Bryan Collier depicts Jimmy's father reading a newspaper article about Emmett Till, the text moves to the eminent conflict between the bus driver and Parks. "'I said give me those seats!' the bus driver bellowed. Mrs. Parks looked up in surprise. The two men on the opposite side of the aisle were rising to move into the crowded black section. Jimmy's father muttered, more to himself than anyone else, 'I don't feel like trouble today. I'm gonna move.'" But Parks resists: "Mrs. Parks stood to let him out, looked at James Blake, the bus driver, and then sat back down." The order to move became the desire to stay, to continue to dream and also to have space to think.

Giovanni writes: "'You better make it easy on yourself!' Blake yelled," to which the response is "'Why do you pick on us?' Mrs. Parks asked with that quiet strength of hers." Giovanni continues, "'I'm going to call the police!' Blake threatened" and is answered, "'Do what you must,' Mrs. Parks quietly replied. She was not frightened. She was not going to give in to that which was wrong." Giovanni masterfully depicts multiple sides of the crisis. "Some of the white people were saying aloud, 'She ought to be arrested,' and 'Take her off this bus.' Some of the black people, recognizing the potential for ugliness, got off the bus. Others stayed on, saying among themselves, 'That is the neutral section. She has a right to be there.'" But most importantly, "Mrs. Parks sat."

Giovanni reiterates that lack of movement with Parks's reflection as she stays put: "As Mrs. Parks sat waiting for the police to come, she thought of all the brave men and women, boys and girls who stood tall for civil rights. She recited in her mind the 1954 Brown versus Board of Education decision, in which the United States Supreme Court ruled that separate is 'inherently unequal.'" Giovanni presents Parks's rationale as well: "She sighed as she realized she was tired. Not tired from work but tired of putting white people first. Tired of stepping off sidewalks to let white people pass, tired of eating at separate lunch counters and learning at separate schools." She continues, "She was tired of 'Colored' entrances, 'Colored' balconies, 'Colored' drinking fountains, and 'Colored' taxis. She was tired of getting somewhere first and being waited on last. Tired of 'separate,' and definitely tired of 'not equal.'"

But finally, Giovanni's representation connects Parks to the generations before her: "She thought about her mother and her grandmother and knew they would want her to be strong. She had not sought this moment, but she was ready for it." Hence, the same response to the police: "When the policeman bent down to ask, 'Auntie, are you going to move?' all the strength of the people through all those many years joined in her. Rosa Parks said no." The stillness in this case, both in Parks's reflection and her resistance to shifting her place, connects with the physical response of those with whom she is in community.

Giovanni wrote, "Jo Ann Robinson was at the Piggly Wiggly when she learned of the arrest. She had stopped in to purchase a box of macaroni and cheese. She always served macaroni and cheese when she baked red snapper for dinner. A sister member of the Women's Political Council approached her just as she reached the checkout lane." Robinson is also in transition from work to home duties but is called into action by this news; it is clear that she is already connected, however, through the Women's Political Council. Her response is immediate: "'Not Mrs. Parks!' Mrs. Robinson exclaimed. She then looked furtively around. 'Pass the word that everybody should meet me at my office at ten o'clock tonight,' she said."

Giovanni continues, "Mrs. Robinson was also Dr. Robinson, a professor at Alabama State, the college designated for 'Colored' people and she was the newly elected president of the Women's Political Council. She rushed home to put dinner on the table, cleaned up the kitchen, and put the kids to bed. She kissed her husband good-bye and hurried to the college. It was dark when they finally gathered." Robinson's narrative as both a professional and educated woman and political activist is significant here. She is also able to care for her family and hold agency in her community as she gathers women in response to Parks' arrest.

The narrative depicts the response both as collective action and a continuation of the movement the women had begun. "The twenty-five women first held hands in prayer in hopes that they were doing the right thing. After all, they were going to use the stencil maker, printer, and paper of Alabama State without permission. If they were caught at the college, they all could be arrested for trespassing. But they were working to undermine a vicious law. They decided they would stand under the umbrella of courage Rosa Parks had offered . . . ." Their *standing* was a continuation of Parks's sitting, with both as effective statements of action. The group makes stencils on machine keys to create "enough posters for almost every citizen of color in Montgomery." Giovanni writes, "The posters read; NO RIDERS TODAY: SUPPORT MRS. PARKS— STAY OFF THE BUSES; WALK ON MONDAY" and continues, "The next morning, as people read the posters, they remembered the joy they felt when the Supreme Court declared that separate was not equal. They were sure that once the highest court in the land had spoken, they would not be treated so badly. But that was not the case."

As Giovanni reiterates the idea that activism is not individual, the text returns to Emmett Till's narrative and the violent attack on his life. "Soon after the ruling, Emmett Till, a fourteen-year-old boy in Money, Mississippi, was viciously lynched. At his funeral, more than one hundred thousand people mourned with his mother. She left his casket open, saying, 'I want the world to see what they did to my boy.' Now, only weeks after his killers were freed, Rosa Parks had taken a courageous stand. The people were ready to stand with her." As Parks *sat*, not just in response to injustice against her but in response to violence against the Black community, others around her *stood*. Giovanni writes, "They came together in a great mass meeting: the Women's Political Council, the NAACP, and all the churches. . . . 'We will stay off the buses,' Dr. King intoned. 'We will walk until justice runs down like water and righteousness like a mighty stream.'" Again, the stasis and calm on the bus with which Parks responds turns into a narrative of physical movement with the Montgomery bus boycott which took place for over a year. Giovanni writes, "And the people walked. They walked in the rain. They walked in the hot sun. They walked early in the morning. They walked late at night. They walked at Christmas, and they walked at Easter. They walked on the Fourth of July; they walked on Labor Day. They walked on Thanksgiving, and then it was almost Christmas again. They still walked."

But Giovanni also depicts the support of the community's efforts as she writes, "People from all over the United States sent shoes and coats and money so that the citizens of Montgomery could walk. Everyone was proud of their nonviolent movement. And the soul force that bound the community together would sustain many marchers for the years of struggle that were yet to come." The movement of the women to Alabama State to begin the protest in response to Parks's arrest in Montgomery connected to the movement of the community to walk and to garner support outside of the city as well.

Giovanni concludes: "On November 13, 1956, almost a year after the arrest of Rosa Parks, the Supreme Court of the United States ruled that segregation on the buses, like segregation at schools, was illegal. Segregation was wrong . . . Rosa Parks said no so that the Supreme Court could remind the nation that the Constitution of the United States makes no provision for second-class citizenship. We are all equal under the law and are all entitled to its protection." With the final statement, "The integrity, the dignity, the quiet strength of Rosa Parks turned her no into a YES for change," like Giovanni's other work in the spirit of change that Parks inspired, this narrative depicts the generational and community strength of Black women to create transformational change.

"In Gratitude for the Dream"

Just a few years after Parks inspired the movement for change to which Giovanni referred, Hansberry dedicated her 1959 *Raisin in the Sun*, a seminal work in African American drama: "To Mama: *in gratitude for the dream*" (6). Citing Langston Hughes, she begins with "What happens to a dream deferred?/Does it dry up/Like a raisin in the sun?/Or fester like a sore—/And then run?/Does it stink like rotten meat/Or crust and sugar over—/Like a syrupy sweet?/Maybe it just sags/Like a heavy load./*Or does it explode?*" (7). In the introduction to the American version of the script, Robert Nemiroff wrote, "Produced in 1959, the play presaged the revolution in black and women's consciousness—and the revolutionary ferment in Africa—that exploded in the years following the playwright's death in 1965 to ineradicably alter the social fabric and consciousness of the nation and the world" (8). Although we focus on Walter Lee's story, centered around his plea "Mama I want so many things," what about his wife Ruth, whose beauty in her early to mid-30s has faded with the labor of existence? What are the dreams for Walter Lee's sister, Beneatha, at twenty, whose radical desire to go to medical school (at a time between World War II and their present day) is challenged by the dreams of her brother and the needs of the family? Beyond the activism taking place in the protests in the mid-1950s in the South, what do liberatory narratives look like in more private spaces?

Nemiroff continues, "much else passed unnoticed in the play at the time, speaks to issues that are now inescapable: value systems of the black family; concepts of African American beauty and identity; class and generational conflicts; the relationships of husbands and wives, black men and women; the outspoken (if then yet unnamed) feminism of the daughter; and, in the penultimate scene between Beneatha and Asagai, the larger statement of the play—and the ongoing struggle it portends" (6). What is that struggle for Beneatha, who has experienced the same loss as her brother?

By setting the play in both a specific and an ambiguous time "Sometime between World War II and the present" but in a specific place, Chicago's South Side (24), Hansberry makes her work about Black girls' dreams both individual and intergenerational. For the female characters, the pursuit of dreams also includes the embracing of intellect and their own identities outside of relationships. Mama is a widow waiting to establish a legacy for the family in her husband's name, and Ruth is positioned in conflict with Walter Lee's desires, but Beneatha is positioned as having dreams of her own. Beneatha, perhaps, has the greatest chance of the three for creating a different path. Nemiroff writes:

> For at the deepest level it is not a specific situation but the human condition, human aspiration, and human relationships—the persistence of dreams, of the bonds and conflicts between men and women, parents and children, old ways and new, and the endless struggle against human oppression, whatever the forms it may take, and for individual fulfillment, recognition, and liberation—that are at the heart of such plays. It is not surprising that in each generation we recognize ourselves in them anew. (14)

In *Raisin*, Hansberry gives readers a glimpse into the ways that pursuit of goals and dreams may or may not lead to liberation for everyone involved.

Hansberry writes: "Ruth is about thirty. We can see that she was a pretty girl, even exceptionally so, but now it is apparent that life has been little that she expected, and disappointment has already begun to hang in her face. In a few years, before thirty-five even, she will be known among her people as a 'settled woman'" (25). Aging becomes a point of contention between Ruth and Walter Lee, who tells her while she was stirring eggs that she looks young but then revokes the compliment: "Just for a second it was—you looked real young again. . . . It's gone now—you look like yourself again" (27). It is clear that his meanness, and even the banter between the two of them, is based on the failure to have their individual and collective dreams realized. Walter Lee wants to go in on liquor store, to which Ruth responds "(*Softly*) Walter, that ain't none of our money" (34). Walter responds, "(*Not listening at all or even looking at her*) This morning, I was lookin' in the mirror and thinking about it. . . . I'm thirty-five years old; I been married eleven years and I got a boy who sleeps in the living room—(*Very, very quietly*)—and all I got to give him is stories about how rich white people live . . . ." (34). With the reminder, to eat, he yells, "DAMN MY EGGS—DAMN ALL THE EGGS THAT EVER WAS!" (34).

To return to Ruth's dream, she has to respond to him first: "(*Wearily*) Honey, you never say nothing new. I listen to you every day, every night and every morning, and you never say nothing new. (*Shrugging*) So you would rather *be* Mr. Arnold than be his chauffeur. So—I would *rather* be living in Buckingham Palace" (34). Walter is unable to see her in order to respond to her desires: "That is just what is wrong with the colored woman in this world. . . . Don't understand about building their men up and making 'em feel like they something. Like they can do something" (34). They continue, with Ruth stating, "(*Drily, but to hurt*) There *are* colored men who do things," to which Walter responds, "No thanks to the colored woman." Ruth retorts," Well, being a colored woman I guess I can't help myself none," (34) as she continues to prepare clothes to iron.

Walter finally mumbles, "We one group of men tied to a race of women with small minds!" (35), but then Beneatha enters as the argument that profound intellect as a younger Black woman is of value to the family collective. "She is about twenty, as slim and intense as her brother. She is not as pretty as her sister-in-law, but her lean, almost intellectual face has a handsomeness of its own" (35). Beneatha's beauty is different from Ruth's and is also marked by her appearance and her speech.

Hansberry writes:

She wears a bright-red flannel nightie, and her thick hair stands wildly about her head. Her speech is a mixture of many things; it is different from the rest of the family's insofar as education has permeated her sense of English—and perhaps the Midwest rather than the south has finally—at last—won out in her inflection; but not altogether, because over all of it is a soft slurring and transformed use of vowels which is the decided influence of the Southside. (35)

As she argues with Walter about paying for medical school, Beneatha exclaims, "I have never asked anyone around here to do anything for me!" (37). However, then she asks, "What do you want from me, Brother—that I quit school or just drop dead, which?" (37).

It is clear that her dreams conflict with her brother's desire for their father's insurance money, as Walter asks, "Who the hell told you you had to be a doctor? If you so crazy 'bout messing 'round with sick people then go be a nurse like other women—or just get married and be quiet." (37). Her intellect is not valued in a narrative that says that masculinity must be at the cost of feminine empowerment, as Beneatha responds: "Well—you finally got it said. . . . It took you three years but you finally got it said. Walter, give up; leave me alone—it's Mama's money" (38). To Walter's assertion over the money as his father's son, she responds, "So what? He was mine, too—and Travis' grandfather—but the insurance money belongs to Mama" (38). In bringing the conversations together, Walter, "(*Looking at his wife and his sister from the door, very sadly*)" calls them "The world's most backward race of people, and that's a fact" (38).

Here, Walter Lee is a reminder that Black masculinity is not necessarily responsible for liberation of either current or future generations but that men and women must be in conversation with each other about collective desires. Beneatha is a reminder that individual demands for freedom do not necessarily coalesce with each other. The text needs the three generations of women—Mama, Ruth, and Beneatha (and even potentially a fourth with the pregnancy)—to reveal the potential and realization of Black girlhood dreams.

In a conversation between Ruth and Mama in which Ruth supports Mama's desire for a new house to move from the "rat trap" they currently inhabit, Mama states, "(*Looking up at the words "rat trap" and then looking around and leaning back and sighing—in a suddenly reflective mood*) "Rat trap"—yes, that's all it is. (*Smiling*). I remember just as well the day me and Big Walter moved in here. Hadn't been married but two weeks and wasn't planning on living here no more than a year. (*She shakes her head at the dissolved dream*)" (45).

Lena Younger continues: "We was going to set away, little by little, don't you know, and buy a little place out in Morgan Park. We had even picked out the house. (*Chuckling a little*). Looks right dumpy today. But Lord, child, you should know all the dreams I had 'bout buying that house and fixing it up and making me a little garden in the back—(*She waits and stops smiling*) And didn't none of it happen. (*Dropping her hands in a futile gesture*)," (45) to which Ruth responds, "(*Keep[ing] her head down, ironing*) Yes, life can be a barrel of disappointments, sometimes" (45). While Ruth reflects on what the family was not able to have or do, Beneatha thinks of the future and what she wants to do.

Beneatha represents another Hughes poem, "Genius Child," in which he wrote, "This is a song for the genius child./Sing it softly, for the song is wild./ Sing it softly as ever you can-/Lest the song get out of hand" and also the collection of writings about her life in *To Be Young, Gifted and Black* (1967). If her story could conclude in an ideal way, it might be that there is room for Black girlhood emerging into womanhood at the top.

> Little girl/Dreaming of a baby grand piano/(Not knowing there's a Steinway bigger, bigger)/Dreaming of a baby grand to play. . . . There's always room/ *They say,*/At the top. (From "To Be Somebody" in *The Collected Poems of Langston Hughes*, p. 374)

Reclaiming Black Girlhood through Performance

Less than a decade before Hansberry envisioned the gifted blackness of Beneatha's dreams, Gwendolyn Brooks's protagonist Maud Martha was trying to define her role in the 1953 novel of the same name, in which Martha wanted "to create—a role, a poem, picture, music, a rapture in stone: great. But not for her. What she wanted was to donate to the world a good Maud Martha. That was the offering, the bit of art, that could not come from any other. She would polish and have that" (164). Martha tries to construct a sense of goodness as art that holds original value that she, and no one else, can produce. Unlike what others were creating—"a poem, picture, music," even stonework—the fictional Martha who remains mired in Maud everydayness, wants to make something better, purely of herself. This Chicago narrative, the Bronzeville of Brooks's own childhood and adolescence, does not exactly mirror the tales of the southern United States represented in other texts of the time, but the period in time represented by Brooks and, later, by Toni Morrison as well, was one of debate over how Black girls would be educated.

For Martha, it was an integrated school. "The school looked solid," (146) Brooks wrote. "Up the street, mixed in the wind, blew the children, and turned the corner onto the brownish-red brick school court. It was wonderful. There were lives in the buildings. Past the tiny lives the children blew. Cramp, inhibition, choke—they did not trouble themselves about these" (147). Children in this scene were children, there solely to secure their education and to play.

> And inevitably the little fellows in kickers, ten, twelve, thirteen years old, nonchalant just for the fun of it—who lingered on the red bricks, throwing balls to each other, or reading newspapers and comic books, or punching each other half playfully.

But eventually every bit of the wind managed to blow itself in, and by five minutes after nine the school court was bare. There was not a hot cap nor a bow ribbon anywhere (148)

Outside of school, however, Martha deals with her grandmother's death, "She who had taken the children of Abraham Brown to the circus, and who had bought them pink popcorn, and Peanut Crinkle candy, who had laughed— that Ernestine was dead" (157). She also struggles to construct a sense of herself both inside and outside what others think. Her practice of equality, for example, is to place a sofa over a hole in her carpet and raise a window as she awaits a visit from her white classmate to refute the idea that "colored people's" homes were not equal to those of whites: "Often it was said that colored people's houses necessarily had a certain heavy, unpleasant smell. Nonsense, that was. Vicious—and nonsense. But she raised every window.

Here was the theory of racial equality about to be put into practice and she only hoped she would be <u>equal to being equal</u>" (159). She expresses concern about her white classmate visiting, lamenting that to Charles, "she was the whole 'colored' race, and Charles was the personalization of the entire Caucasian plan" (160).

Even changing for Charles, however, makes Martha feel as if she is seeking racial benevolence, which causes a different feeling for her: "What was this she was feeling now? Not fear, not fear. A sort of gratitude! It sickened her to realize it. As though Charles, in coming, gave her a gift. . . . Recipient and benefactor. It's so good of you. You're being so good" (160).

Goodness is what Martha struggles with, as she decides by age sixteen, watching a performance by artist Howie Joe, "She was going to keep herself to herself. She did not want fame. She did not want to be a 'star'" (163).

Even being ordinary required effort, if not excellence, for the fictional Martha and real children like her. In 1940, in Charlotte Hawkins Brown's *The Correct Thing to Do, to Say, to Wear*, the messaging was that behavior, speech, and dress could and would determine the pathways of young girls' lives. In 1941, the year in which Morrison set her inaugural novel *The Bluest Eye*, the system of education served to supplement the system or care that held Pecola in the MacTeer home after her father's abuse of her mother and of her placed her "outdoors." For Claudia MacTeer, "outdoors was the new terror of life" after Pecola was placed with her family by the county. They had fun "concentrate(ing) on helping our guest not feel outdoors" (17). But that still did not help Pecola escape her traumatic situation and succeed at the center and not on the margins of mainstream narratives. She was still not able to play, to enjoy childhood in the way that other children did without worrying about verbal attacks based on her family situation or even threats that remained from physical and sexual assault.

Freedom, Play, and Reproductive Liberation

Ntozake Shange's *for colored girls who have considered suicide/when the rainbow is enuf*, in which she determined that 1955 "is not a good year for little blk girls" is published and performed just a few years later in 1975 and 1976. In the groundbreaking work that includes monologues of seven women marked only by a solid color, Shange is also able to dictate the terms into which a Black girl might enter the world and thrive. She answers the query of what it meant to sing a song intentionally and exclusively for "colored girls." These texts, birthed from the Black Arts movement, reclaim Black womanhood and girlhood as a means of illustrating their connected journeys toward liberation.

The lady in brown opens *for colored girls* by detailing the context of the choreopoem. It will be made up of: "dark phrases of womanhood/of never havin been a girl" (3). The dreams one might have as a girl are cut short from the very inception of this poem and, one might argue, eliminated entirely. Rather than dreams, then, we have cries for help. "i can't hear anything/but maddening screams/& the soft strains of death," she argues, "& you promised me/you promised me . . . ." (3). The reader lingers with the possibility of the promise here along with the question: What is the burden that is being reckoned with, and by whom? The answer is a song: "somebody/anybody/sing a black girl's song/bring her out/to know herself/to know you/but sing her rhythms/carin/struggle/hard times" (3). Shange is asking, through the speaker, who can sing that song that will let a black girl see herself in music and in rhythm—the "carin/struggle [and] hard times?" Shange is also asking for a lullaby, and the fact that the text is a musical is also her response. She is asking for a text that will replace the "maddening screams" and "strains of death."

Finally, she is asking for true representation of "a black girl's song": "sing her song of life/she's been dead so long/closed in silence so long/she doesn't know the sound/of her own voice/her infinite beauty/she's half-notes scattered/without rhythm/no tune/sing her sighs/sing the song of her possibilities/sing a righteous gospel/let her be born/let her be born/& handled warmly" (4–5). Returning to one of the foundational platforms of the book, this text is both a requiem (act or token of remembrance) for the girl who has not been allowed to grow and flourish and a lullaby for those still being born into the world. The argument to both "let her be born" and imperative to "handle [her] warmly" are part of a poetics of reproductive liberation. The requiem is generally a song for the dead, but Shange's interpretation is that the power of the song can bring her back. She has been represented as half-notes, without the rhythm or the tune that will illustrate an accurate picture, and the request is to emphasize her possibilities instead. A "righteous gospel" can right the representation of girlhood through text. Finally, the imperative to let her be born (repeated twice) and be handled warmly signifies a rebirth that will change the narrative of her life.

This poem, I argue, is a both a song of the lives of Black women and girls and a metaphor about reproduction as liberation for Black girls. Shange asks not just that the girl be born but also that she be born with possibility. As she notes, *for colored girls* is poetry, music, and theater all at once, created from process, and so, this requiem for the loss of Shange is also represented as a celebration of the creative genius that she brought into the world that lasted (continues to last) for decades since. Therefore, this piece is also not conceived haphazardly, but while intentionally thinking of community.

In the histories of the text, when Shange wrote that she met collaborators Jessica and Nashira "thru [*sic*] Third World Communications (The Woman's Collective) when the first anthology of Third World women writers in the U.S.A. was published" (ix): "San Francisco waz inundated with women poets, women's readings, & a multilingual woman presence, new to all of us & desperately appreciated" (ix). This is community, not the isolation of an academic space. That community included their roles as mothers, daughters, grandmothers ("as women"). She adds that, at the same time, Shameless Hussy Press and The Oakland Women's Press Collective were also reading "anywhere and everywhere they could," adding, "This is the energy & part of the style that nurtured *for colored girls* . . . " (x). But this energy and these presses were also in conversation with academic spaces. Additionally, it allows for a different type of intellectual intuition, as Shange acknowledges how she comes to understand herself as text, including her mind, her body, and spirit:

> Knowing a woman's mind & spirit had been allowed me, with dance I discovered my body more intimately than I had imagined possible. With the acceptance of the ethnicity of my thighs & backside, came a clearer understanding of my voice as a woman & as a poet. . . . Just as Women's Studies had rooted me to an articulated female heritage & imperative. . . . (xi)

for colored girls, then, is a reclaiming and a rebirth of the types of work that center (and, note, are not centered in) women's studies and, specifically, the necessity of using Black women's writing as the center. The reclaiming of us and of our "stuff" is the poem and the text. The form is fluid, as it began as seven poems about seven "different kinds of women."

The central argument here is that community is the movement toward liberation. I am also not interested in finding a starting point of communal liberation, at least in this piece, but the not-always-collaborative herstories of women's/black women's liberation certainly inform this moment. What does it mean, then, to focus on the circle of women who complete the narrative that begins with literal and metaphorical Black girlhood? Can freedom from difficult, and even tragic, circumstances be claimed through the telling? Can liberation be present with the pain that is also evident throughout this narrative? Both? As with the multiple narratives present in *for colored girls*, we can and should do all of the above.

Like many other Black women writers and artists of the mid-1970s, Ntozake Shange was concerned with centering not only the experiences but also the survival of Black women. In celebrating their lives as art, she also reclaims their abilities to tell their stories even from their youth. Through the women, the "colored" girls are able to play again. There is a game of tag and then hand games that bring them together:

> mama's little baby likes shortnin, shortnin,
> mama's little baby likes shortnin bread
> mama's little baby likes shortnin, shortnin,
> mama's little baby likes shortnin bread
> little sally walker, sittin in a saucer
> rise, sally, rise, wipe your weepin eyes
> an put your hands on your hips
> an let your backbone slip
> o, shake it to the east
> o, shake it to the west
> shake it to the one
> that you like the best. (6)

The game ends with the lady in purple stating, "you're it" (6). The "you" could be any of the women here, as is noted with both the cycle of stories and the random selection of who is "in" and "out" in the games. Tag and hand-clapping games are both strategy and narrative, as there can be a different "chosen" person each time. These interactions bring the women together and give them each a chance to tell their own stories. This recollection of child's play is a transition into letting the women sing their own songs from childhood to coming of age. The stories, for the girls turned women, represent the liberation of not just being born but also being able to grow up on their own terms. *They are singing their songs from childhood to coming of age* that begin with narratives of Black girlhood and move through discussions of agency and sexuality, from "graduation nite" into a final narrative on sexuality that reclaims that aspect of sexual freedom from a young age, as the lady in brown expresses her love for Haitian revolutionary Toussaint L'Ouverture.

The lady in brown narrates: "TOUSSAINT L'OUVERTURE/became my secret lover at the age of 8/i entertained him in my bedroom/widda flashlight under my covers/way inta the night/we discussed strategies/how to remove white girls from my hopscotch games/& etc." (27). Toussaint [some of his story] helps her to come up with her own escape plan after the decision to integrate her school.

She states: "TOUSSAINT/waz layin in bed wit me next to raggedy ann/ the night I decided to run away from my/integrated home/integrated street/ integrated school/1955 waz not a good year for lil blk girls" (27). In this narrative, which details 1955 (the year when Emmett Till was murdered, the year when the Montgomery bus boycotts began, and a year that was not good for black children in general or, specifically, "lil blk girls," even in a society that was seemingly moving toward more equal rights for them), the full story allows the lady in brown to strategize by finding a friend in Toussaint as an ideal "secret lover" but then actualized by meeting just an ordinary boy. Shange follows the narrative of the young girl who follows Toussaint L'Ouverture to Toussaint Jones, and then Toussaint Jones to the banks of the river where her own narrative pronounces, which can be imagined, that 1955 was "not a good year for little blk girls."

When we think of 1955—when the Montgomery bus boycotts began in December, and even earlier, when Emmett Till was murdered in August—we can think of a general mourning of the loss of a Black boy's life and the hardship of those who braved the cold for their own rights. The lady in purple's narrative reminds us, however, that Emmett Till's mother, and the mothers, sisters, daughters of all who were suffering restrictions on their own liberation, were not allowed access to their childhood dreams either.

Dreams become a trope in Black women's writing and specifically referencing Black girlhood. The lady in brown states: "Toussaint said 'lets go to haiti'/I said 'awright'/& packed some very important things in a brown paper bag/so i wdnt haveta come back" (28). She walks with her invisible revolutionary through North St. Louis with plans to "stow away/on a boat for new orleans/& catch a creole fishin-rig for port-au-prince" (28), when an "ol young boy" yells at her to come to him. The lady in brown responds as to her dilemma whether to stow away with the revolutionary Toussaint or engage with her peer: "I mumbled to L'OUVERTURE/'what shd I do'/finally/i asked this silly ol boy/'WELL WHO ARE YOU?'" (28). She continues: "he say/'MY NAME IS TOUSSAINT JONES'/well/i looked right at him/those skidded out corduroy pants/ a striped teashirt wid holes in both elbows/a new scab over his left eye/& i said/'what's yr name again'/he say/'i'm toussaint jones'/'wow/I am on my way to see/TOUSSAINT L'OUVERTURE in HAITI" (28).

As the lady in brown continues to talk with Toussaint Jones, who invites her to the docks to look at the boats, she is saddened by the feeling that Toussaint L'Ouverture is leaving, until she realizes: "TOUSSAINT JONES waznt too different/from TOUSSAINT L'OUVERTURE/cept the ol one waz in haiti/& this one wid me speakin English & eatin apples/yeah./toussaint jones waz awright wit me/no tellin what all spirits we cd move/down by the river/st. louis 1955" (1930). The narrative ends, then, with a choice to shift attention from an imagined muse to someone she can share actual time with. This story, then, rewrites a coming-of-age narrative of loneliness and isolation into one with potential for liberation and even revolutionary partnership.

A final argument for the power of coming-of-age narratives in *for colored girls* deals with rebirth to be able to express true emotions as a "colored girl." The lady in orange's "requiem [*sic*] for myself/cuz I have died in a real way," begins: "i had convinced myself colored girls had no right to sorrow/& i lived & loved that way & kept sorrow on the curb/allegedly for you/but i know i did it for myself/i cdnt stand it/i cdnt stand bein sorry & colored at the same time/it's so redundant in the modern world" (43). The lady in purple follows: "i want you to love me/let me love you/i don't wanna dance with ghosts/ snuggle lovers i made up in my drunkenness/lemme love you just like i am/a colored girl/i'm finally bein real/no longer symmetrical & impervious to pain" (44). The two narratives that these monologues rewrite are that colored girls have a right to feel sorry and do feel pain. They want to love and to feel loved as well.

As none of the narratives have easy conclusions, the question of whether this destiny can be taken into the next generation is present and even challenged in the "beau willie" monologue of *for colored girls*. The lady in red recounts: "& crystal went & got pregnant again/beau most beat her to death when she tol him/she still gotta scar/under her right tit where he cut her up/still crystal went right on & had the baby/so now beau willie had two children/a little girl/naomi kenya & a boy/Kwame beau willie brown/& there was no air" (56)

In this beginning to a story that will end tragically, air represents breath. The children belong not only to crystal but to beau willie, starting with a little girl and a boy featuring names that represent their heritage and even their father's name. As the narrative continues, crystal obtains a court order and beau willie becomes more violent, swinging chairs as he declares a wish to marry her so he could stop drivin "them crazy spics round" (58?). The narrative then shifts to a first-person narrative told by crystal (but possibly also by "red" in an omniscient voice): "i stood by beau in the window/with naomi reachin for me/& kwame screamin mommy mommy from the fifth story/but I cd only whisper/& he dropped em" (60).

The power and pain of this moment suggests that even the telling does not reclaim the lives of these children. As the women examine the story, the conversation is about what they could have done to change the story. The lady in red states, "I waz missin something," to which the lady in purple adds, "something so important," the lady in orange adds, "something promised," and the lady in purple adds, "makin me whole" (61). The words and phrases continue—the lady in orange: "sense," the lady in green: "pure," and the lady in blue concludes: "all the gods comin into me/layin me open to myself" (61).

What had been missing all the time was the ability to tell and to continue their stories. What had been missing was the ability to feel whole, to make sense of both the triumphs and tragedies in their lives, and to truly see and feel themselves. Through Shange, through these women handling each other, the readers, and themselves with honesty and care, came the ability to return the girlhood and sense of identity that had been missing. They, and we, are the colored girls the world has been looking for.

Interlude

The CROWN Act highlights years of workplace hair discrimination finally being legally reprehensible.

—Amiah Taylor, *Fortune* magazine (March 21, 2022)

I t is March 2022, and Judge Ketanji Brown Jackson is undergoing the third day of confirmation hearings in the US Senate to become the first African American woman Supreme Court Justice of the United States. Jackson was born in Washington, DC, and educated in Florida, graduating from Miami Palmetto Senior High School in Pinecrest, Florida, and then attending Harvard University and Harvard Law School. Not uncritically, it is important to mention that she has held the vice chair of the US Sentencing Commission before serving as a federal judge on the US Court of Appeals for the District of Columbia Circuit since 2021.

At the same time, the United States just passed legislation by the House of Representatives on Friday, March 18, in a vote of 235 to 189 toward addressing Black natural hair as a point of discrimination in employment and education. The CROWN (Creating a Respectful and Open World for Natural Hair) Act, which was first introduced to Congress in March 2019, "prohibits prejudicial treatment towards individuals on the basis of their hair texture or hairstyle." At the time of this writing, the bill now goes to the Senate. On *Good Morning America*, in March 2022, US Rep. Shontel Brown (D) of Ohio stated, "It is important that we put something in place so that hair discrimination can no longer exist." At this pivotal moment in American history, Black women are hypervisible in activism and movements for their own benefit, being asked to work magic even as we still demand that people #SayHerName and recognize her #BlackGirlMagic.

Representatives such as Shontel Brown are carrying the torch of those who came before them, from Shirley Chisholm to Sheila Jackson Lee, of Texas, who has served since 1995. There are a number of issues that can and still be addressed, from Black girlhood and health (including mental health) to education. As we speak, mental health is still being negotiated and talked around. Compound this with everything brought into and from these narratives. What remains is a will to survive.

Chapter 4

Create

On Radical Creativity as a Movement

We never forget to say thank you to the ancestors . . . our blessings
in the stars.

—Beyoncé, *Black Is King*

W hat are the legacies of civil rights for those who are experiencing
their own journeys in a contemporary era? How do they, do we,
remember and tell their stories?

The movement for Black girls, then, is from individual to collective whole
identities. Shange suggested that these shifts take place as part of a communal
effort with connections first as children and then as adult women. The movement from civil rights into Black Power/Black Arts is also one of creative engagement as radical liberation. It is from Langston Hughes's question of what
happens to a "dream deferred" to Lorraine Hansberry's *Raisin in the Sun,* to
the tragic representations of four little Black girls murdered in Birmingham
at the Sixteenth Street Baptist Church, among other tragedies throughout African American histories. It is also, however, a movement toward a Black girl
renaissance when we can also ask the question: How do we come to celebrate
Black girls?

What brings Black girls joy? How do we acknowledge positive experiences
and milestones while projecting what may change? What are the narratives
of community, commemoration, and celebration? Additionally, what and
where were protest movements rooted for girls in their own homes? What did
protection look like? How does physical violence also connect to emotional
violence and assaults on their possibility?

These narratives are not always liberatory, as we look to texts such as *The
Bluest Eye* and *Push* as texts that mark when girlhood was arrested and failed,
in addition to liberatory potential, to move through trauma. Radical creativity

becomes both a way to gain or regain agency and celebrate who Black girls are and even, at times, just to see them and their stories.

Radical creativity becomes a way to reimagine Black women's experiences and for them to liberate those experiences from how we think about revolutionary expressions of African American identities through masculinity. This is a requiem, then, for the narratives of the Black girls who have been lost in transmission and also a rebirth for those whose stories have been and are being reimagined and carried forward.

Rebirth

> We dream of different ways of being, of existing. For Isie and Janie, who want to travel the world and escape bounds of girlhood and domesticity. For Pecola, whose eyes can never be blue enough to escape what she has seen. For Claireece "Precious" Jones, who wants to be more than an illiterate teenage mother and incest victim. These stories are for girls whose have yet to achieve the play of their dreams.
>
> —"Building Worlds of Our Dreams," J. Lewis, *South: A Scholarly Journal*

In *The Bluest Eye*, Morrison reaches into her own childhood to find a point of origin for Pecola's desire for beauty, one rooted in the ugliness she sees in her daily life. Pecola, the character, does not have a chance for existence, as she is outcast from the community; left, as Langston Hughes wrote, a "brokenwinged bird" that cannot fly. In her poem "To the Young Who Want to Die," Gwendolyn Brooks issues instructions that bring us back to Ntozake Shange's *for colored girls who have considered suicide/when the rainbow is enuf.* Brooks wrote: "Sit down. Inhale. Exhale./The gun will wait. The lake will wait./The tall gall in the small seductive vial/will wait will wait:/will wait a week: will wait through April./You do not have to die this certain day" (in *Children of Promise* 115). In a reminder that death is always a plausible end, especially for Black youths, Brooks continues, "Death can/attend to you tomorrow. Or next week. Death is/just down the street; is most obliging neighbor;/can meet you any moment." But her poem ends with the hopefulness of staying: "You need not die today./Stay here—through pout or pain or peskyness./Stay here. See what the news is going to be tomorrow/Graves grow no green that you can use./Remember, green's your color. You are Spring" (*Children of Promise* 115). Black girls have been present, have been writing into womanhood, and have been contributing to and speaking out about the progress of their people.

Where I Sit

Here is the seat
Where somebody sat
Before me.
Someone who looks like me.
Where they didn't stand up
Because someone said so
Even when that someone who was supposed to serve them
Said no.
Where they had to look at the hatred
That resonated with difference
Just because of the color of our skin and our nation's
Tone.—j. b. lewis

For most people, their exposure to Black communities and Black literature is largely ordained by what they have been taught in public schools or by understanding some principal moments in the civil rights movement. One case in particular, *Swann v. Charlotte-Mecklenburg Board of Education* (1971), evokes a fair amount of contention and passion regarding its status as a landmark case to have inspired mandatory integrated busing. Keeping that importance in regard, it is also imperative to acknowledge the lack of headway in the means of desegregating.

The legacy of *Brown* is still referred to in great detail, yet what is the accountability for the conditions toward greater justice and equity in education in Charlotte? In their 2014 article "Segregation Revisited," authors Abiola A. Farinde, Tempestt Adams, and Chance W. Lewis recommend looking to the sources of inequity, including the more recent cases of *Swann* and *Melchionni* as representations for what created barriers in public education in Charlotte-Mecklenburg schools. At the time of the article's publication, the authors suggested that true integration and equity had not been achieved and that efforts were actually going in the opposite direction because of the end of intentional efforts. They compared three schools with over sixty percent Black students to three in the mostly white suburban South Charlotte, which had fewer than twenty-six percent Black or nonwhite students to demonstration the inequity in performance and access.

At this point in 2021, during a continued racial pandemic that was heightened with reports of the tragic deaths of several Blacks that circulated during the global pandemic of COVID-19, history is also marked by a pushback against discussions of social justice and critical race theory in education by legislatures including North Carolina, Tennessee, and Florida.

The summer of 2020 and well into 2021, as we navigated the COVID-19 pandemic that still threatens our state, nation, and world and the not-new crises manifest in anti-Black violence that became more visible with the murders of Ahmaud Arbery, Breonna Taylor, Tony McDade, George Floyd, and others, students of African American and Black diasporic descent were caught at a cross-section of crises as they attempted to learn remotely from home during both.

Although remote learning protected their health, the struggle for most school systems and educators to adapt curricular practices and navigate the economic and even the health impact of the pandemic became a theoretical source of research and discussion (with the work of Dr. Bettina Love, *We Want to Do More than Survive* and others) and also revealed the contextual histories of Black education and freedom in America. In my own home, my husband, a high school and college educator, and I tried to teach our own elementary-school-age children what they were supposed to know (per public educational standards) but also what it meant to navigate Black childhood in America during ongoing crises such as these.

In my own educational practice at home, in research and speaking engagements on parents talking to children about race, I put together book lists for adults, children, and families to encourage and provide context for these conversations and researched and reflected on how "motherschooling" can help to support Black children with their own histories, agency, and empowerment. Along with the impact of the digital divide on Black families and the local impact as well (Mecklenburg County, for example, purchased one million dollars' worth of hotspots, after which there was then a great deal of discussion about how to use them without children having to sit on or near hot buses before many students finally went back to in-person learning in November with the ongoing pandemic), there will continue to be a gap discovered and navigated for those who fell between the cracks of society, even here in Charlotte and surrounding areas. There is an ongoing need for educational research and policy that intervenes and offers continued support for parents who want their children to thrive.

I argue that attention is still necessary, not just to the possibilities for racial justice offered by *Brown* and related cases but also to the challenges that subsequent cases posed, which arrested access to equitable educational resources. As discussions of justice and equity are also increased in many organizational structures (including K–12 and higher educational units and industries attempting to "bounce back" from the effects of the pandemic), we offer from the lens of public higher education that an interdisciplinary focus is needed to see what effects still resonate from the journey through, and even the repeal from, the integration of public institutions. Ultimately, these cases still matter, because if equitable education is a destination, we are not "there" yet. We cannot reach equity and justice in society without looking at and addressing problems in public education and educational institutions that serve as models for the access that society needs to see realized.

On Whose and Where We Are

Representing Sojourner Truth's statement in 1851 that "I am a women's rights," these girls then women writers and narrators draw from the lessons of those who came before while creating new legacies of activism. They also represent Anna Julia Cooper's declaration that "Only the black woman can say 'when and where I enter, in the quiet, undisputed dignity of my womanhood, without violence and without suing or special patronage, then and there the whole . . . race enters with me" (*A Voice from the South*, 1894). As the race enters, we must think about the baggage that is carried from Black girlhood into womanhood. Specifically, how are Black girls speaking out and dealing with mental health and issues of their general well-being?

A contemporary example is found in Angie Thomas's *On the Come Up*, in which Brianna navigates her mother's with the help of her strict teacher, Mrs. Murray, her aunt, and her microphone. Brianna is described by her hair, Sisterlocks, and the rest of her "hidden behind her Nikki Giovanni book," with poetry named as her religion, and it is also Brianna's role at Midtown School of the Arts that helps keep her on the right path. Mrs. Murray names Brianna's distraction as she waits for a call about her performance, although she tries "too hard," but Brianna finally tells her that she is waiting for DJ Hype to tell her she can battle in Jimmy's Boxing Ring, known as "The Ring."

"I know you've got skills. I've read your poetry. I just didn't know you wanted to be a rapper," Mrs. Murray says, to which Brianna responds, "I've been rapping since I was ten, but I've never really put myself out there with it . . . let's be real: Your mom saying you're a good rapper is like your mom saying you're cute when you look a hot mess. . . . Maybe I'm good, I don't know. I've been waiting for the right moment" (9). Mrs. Murray encourages her to improve her grades, naming her brother Trey, who graduated from college with honors, although he moved back home and is making pizzas as he searches for a job. Brianna tells her, "I'm gonna improve my grades, I swear. . . . I just gotta do this battle first and see what happens." (11).

Brianna's mother, Jay, is enrolled in a social work degree program and takes classes several nights a week to "make sure other people get the help that she didn't back when she was on drugs" (13). Calling Brianna "Li'l Bit," she questions her about her day, including the practice ACT tests, and tells her that she needs to take schoolwork more seriously. Brianna reflects, "It's not that I don't wanna go to college. I honestly don't know. The main thing I want is to make rapping happen. I do that, it'll be better than any good job a college degree could give me" (15). Jay also tells her daughter that she is "stubborn like [her] daddy, smart-mouthed like [her] daddy, and hotheaded like [her] daddy." Brianna narrates, "I don't have Jay's high cheekbones or her lighter eyes, and I only get her complexion when I stay out in the summer sun all day." She continues, "Sometimes I catch her staring at me, like she's looking for herself. Or like she sees Dad and can't look away" (16). Jay tells her daughter, "Be patient. . . . If he does call, go to the gym, do your li'l battle— . . . and come straight home" (16), warning her not to hang out with Jay's sister "Aunt Pooh." Aunt Pooh is also a support network, telling Jay that the "Sky's the limit," taken from a Biggie Smalls/Notorious B.I.G. song (20). Jay and Pooh's parents died when they were children, and Jay reared her younger sister, as Pooh becomes parental to Brianna.

On the Come Up is connected to the story in *The Hate U Give*. The scene is a year after the murder of Khalil in *The Hate U Give*, and Brianna states, "He was unarmed, but the grand jury decided not to charge the officer. There were riots and protests for weeks. Half the businesses in the Garden were either intentionally burned down by rioters or were casualties of the war. Club Envy, the usual Thursday nightspot, was a casualty" (22). As Brianna follows Aunt Pooh to the entrance through metal detectors (where guns are returned once The Ring ends), bouncers ask Brianna if she is "carrying the torch for Law," her father. "Not really. More like making my own torch and carrying it. I say, 'Yeah,' though, because that's what I'm supposed to say. It's part of being royalty" (23). As other characters find their senses of identity through the written word, Brianna finds hers through performance. "Nothing's been the same since Nas told me the world was mine. Old as that album was back then, it was like waking up after being asleep my whole life. It was damn near spiritual. . . . I fiend for that feeling. It's the reason I rap" (25). She has memorized her dad's music but is taken out of her element when a rapper named Milez, the son of her father's former manager, Supreme, brings up her father's murder in a freestyle line as his father laughs. Brianna reflects, "I wish I had that. Not an asshole for a dad, but my dad. At this point I'd settle for good memories," remembering the night her father was murdered in front of the family's old house while leaving for date night. The story has it that he wasn't in a gang but got caught between the drama of the Garden Disciples and the Crowns who took him out" (35). Brianna's rules come from the battle, knowing your opponent's weakness, using circumstances to your advantage, and "if there's a beat, make sure your flow fits it like a glove" (36–37). She has to leave what she is supposed to do and be outside The Ring to win. "I gotta go for the kill. Here I am, going at him as if I don't have any manners" (39).

From her father's death and mother's subsequent drug use, which leaves Brianna and her brother, Trey, with their grandparents, music becomes her high, but she still has to explain her failure in school.

"The ladies of hip-hop watch from the wall beside my bed . . . from MC Lyte to Missy Elliott to Nicki Minaj to Rapsody . . . the list goes on and on. I figure if I wanna be a queen, queens should watch over me when I sleep." (48) Brianna adds "Shout-out to Michelle Obama. That health kick of hers made the school take the good stuff from the vending machines and made my business very lucrative," as she sells snacks to buy new boots. Brianna still goes through growing pains, putting lip gloss on and debating whether she wants to kiss her friend Malik while wrestling. She experiences what is discussed in Monique Morris's *Pushout*, as she is recorded for not handing over the bag (which doesn't beep) because of her candy stash.

"He grabs my arm again and pulls it behind me. The other one goes behind me too. I try to yank and tug away, which only makes his grip tighter. Before I know it, my chest hits the ground first, then my face is pressed against the cold floor" (60). Tate, the security officer at Brianna's school, calls her a "li'l hoodlum," and the text continues:

> I can't say a word.
> He's not a cop.
> He doesn't have a gun.
> But I don't wanna end up like that boy.
> I want my mom.
> I want my dad.
> I wanna go home. (60)

Brianna discovers that Jay has lost her job when her principal's office calls. Jay demands to know why Brianna is handcuffed and will not talk until she is released. The principal explains that she has sold candy on campus but that there will be an investigation, adding "The guards treat all of the students the same," (65) and calling Brianna "argumentative and aggressive" (66). She has been previously cited for an "outburst" for asking why they never talk about Black people before slavery in history class in addition to having incidents in theater and in fiction class. Her mother Jay tells her to promise she will do as she is told if such a situation as being asked to turn over her bag ever happens again. Jay says, "Bad things can happen, baby. People like that sometimes abuse their power" (69) and adds, "'I need you to act as if you don't have any [power]. Once you're safely out of the situation, *then* we'll handle it. But I need you *safely* out of the situation" (69). Brianna relates this to her talk about the cops: "Do whatever they tell you to do, she said. Don't make them think you're a threat. Basically, weaken myself and take whatever's thrown at me so I can survive that moment" (69). Jay advises Bri to keep her mouth shut for two more years so as not to risk expulsion (69), adding (to Brianna's question about speaking up for herself): "You pick your battles. . . . Not everything deserves a comment or an eye roll or an attitude," and noting, "girls like you are the only ones getting hits on their permanent record!" (70). Like Starr Carter in *The Hate U Give*, Brianna is sent to Midtown to keep from going to Garden High, the neighborhood school.

Jay states: "You think the guards are bad at Midtown? They have actual cops at Garden High. . . . The damn school is treated like a prison. They don't set anybody up to succeed. Say what you want about Midtown, but you've got a better chance there." (70). Jay has lost her job because the church where she worked had to adjust its budget to pay for repairs from the riot (71). She tells Bri that God's got them and that she and Trey are handling it. "I'm fine," Brianna says, to which Jay responds, "No, you're not. It's okay if you're not. You do know you don't have to be strong all the time, right?" (73). Brianna's constant struggle is one over her circumstances, and in this and other moments, she feels like she is drowning and does not know how to control anything happening to and around her (74).

Another of a few books to address mental health in Black girlhood is the novel, *Who Put This Song On?* by writer and poet Morgan Parker. It tells the story of high school student Morgan, who is in a place of "in between" at a predominantly white Christian school but feeling like she does not want to fit in, as she also struggles to embrace her own sexuality, sitting next to someone she likes at the movies (who wants to just be friends) but engaging in oral intercourse with a classmate who asks her to leave the movies with him but also makes her Blackness hypervisible. Morgan feels trapped in many ways; begins therapy after a summer attempted suicide attempt; and finds solace in her friends, dating one of their cousins (Sean), and helping another friend through her own mental health crisis.

Parker shapes the narrative from the beginning as being one that neither ignores mental wellness nor erases a character's problems in seeking it. An early impactful chapter, "This Is a Story About Me," begins, "This is a story about me, and I am the hero of it" (3), even as Morgan sits in the waiting room at her therapist's office, "a place that [she] hate[s]" (3). She constantly questions her difference and tells her therapist, Susan, "I can't get happy," (5) as the narrative describes her "chest . . . welling up with everything [she's] been trying to stuff into [her] mind's closet" (5). As the text continues, Morgan also fights against her history teacher's erasure of her and her history, as she channels Zora Neale Hurston in fashion sense and Harriet Tubman's radical activism on a pop quiz.

> Unsatisfied with the usual blurb on Harriet Tubman from our Christian school textbook, I decided to do some more research. Turns out she was a boss. In addition to being a fugitive during the civil war (the "Moses" Mr. K's looking for, with extra credit for Exodus), Harriet Tubman was also a nurse, a cook, a scout, and a spy for the American government. She also carried a gun and vowed to use it on anyone in the way of her freedom. We never learn any of that in school. (217)

Frustrated that she doesn't get the "truth" about Black women's stories, Morgan doesn't write anything on the quiz out of protest, even pretending to write as the text states, "I'm just not in the mood to play along" (217). She receives in-school detention for not completing the assignment, which leads her to later stage a teach-in about the Black Panther Party's Free Breakfast Program, serving her classmates pancakes outside of the chapel as she tells them about the program. She also charges a dollar for them to touch her hair, for all of the times they have done so without permission (282). To a charge that the Panthers were terrorist, Morgan responds:

> They protected their people and their neighborhoods! They stood up for themselves and their rights! They wanted revolution because they were tired of getting so much less than anyone else, of being beaten and shot by the cops who were supposed to be protecting them. That's why they had education programs and organized their communities. They had to protect themselves, help each other, right? Does that sound like terrorism? (284)

Morgan continues, "I'm energized by the attention, by my own command over the crowd. I can't believe how good it feels to be heard instead of gawked at" (284). Before being sent back to the principal's office, where she is suspended through Christmas break, she has a small moment of validation. This changes soon, as she sits in the car with the "weight" of the sentence: "I feel red-hot and tiny. The familiar slump descends upon my shoulders, and all my worst critics take the stage in my lead. *How could you be so reckless? What were you thinking? What is the point? Who do you think you are?*" (287). She is filled with "fears and complaints and worst-case scenarios" as she tears up her posters, continuing, "Part of me thinks I'll never come back here, and the other, more terrified part knows I will" (288). Another teacher returns a paper to her, titled "The Black Girl Speaks of Rivers: Finding Myself in Langston Hughes and Assata Shakur," along with affirmation that it is "worth something" (288). Morgan reflects, "It is a tremendously excellent essay, even if it's completely wrong for this place. . . . If I were the school, I might kick me out too" (289). Hers is a powerful reflection between feeling right in her own identity but rejected by others:

> I am not understood. I do not belong. No one can ever fully get my jokes or understand what I'm trying to say. Not even Susan, not even my parents, not even my invented versions of Harriet Tubman/my future self. They probably never have. . . . Everyone probably takes pity on me, rolls their eyes when I leave the room, secretly shakes their heads about how it's too bad I'm so weird and I'm not white. (289)

Being a Map

Redemption comes in community from friends, and Parker ends the text with tips for how to share and encourage therapy, and she reflects on her life in the Author's Note (following the concluding chapter, "If You Don't Have a Map, Make a Map of Yourself" (312). She notes, "I didn't get the guy. There was no guy. I don't even remember who I was talking about. They didn't matter. . . . I also didn't lead a social or political revolution. I'm not secretly Toni Morrison or Angela Davis. But . . . I know where I've been, and I know what I want to say to the world. I know my flaws; I know what hurts me and why. And I know what makes me beautiful. Even when other people might not" (315).

Wounds That "Never Heal"

Pulitzer Prize winner Natasha Trethewey's *Memorial Drive: A Daughter's Memoir* (2020) deals with trauma (in handling the death of the author's mother by murder at her stepfather's hands) as Trethewey begins: "Three weeks after my mother is dead I dream of her: We walk a rutted path, an oval track around which we are making our slow revolution: side by side, so close our shoulders nearly touch, neither of us speaking, both of us in our traces. Though I know she is dead I have a sense of contentment, as if she's only gone someplace else to which I've journeyed to meet her. . . . Even in the dream I know what he has done, and yet I smile, lifting my hand and speaking a greeting as he passes. It's then that my mother turns to me, then that I see it: a hole, the size of a quarter, in the center of her forehead" (3).

Describing the scene of violence, Trethewey tries to interrupt what she already knows will happen: "This time I think I can save her. Is it enough to throw myself in the bullet's path? Shout 'No!'? I wake to that single word, my own voice wrenching me from sleep. But it's my mother's voice that remains, her last question to me—'Do you know what it means to have a wound that never heals?'—a refrain" (3).

Trethewey's mother was killed in Atlanta at the age of forty after leaving an abusive relationship with her husband, Trethewey's stepfather, "Big Joe." She recounts in the text letters on a legal pad referencing the Council for Battered Women that she knew that she would get out of her marriage of ten years, and his reactions got worse once he got a gun. She realized after two months of therapy (with him) that she wanted out immediately and the fury that ensued. Trethewey's mother called Rena Bishop at the Council for Battered Women and was referred to an attorney; she then left for a shelter, where her narrative ends. Trethewey writes, "she must have still had hope—if not absolute faith—that her story was a story of escape, of starting anew, that there was a happy ending still ahead of her, that she was indeed living it" (140). At one point, this ending involved new photographs. In the Prologue, she describes the last image of her mother, which was taken shortly before her death:

> She was forty years old. For the sitting she'd chosen a long-sleeved black sheath, the high collar open at the throat. She does not look at the camera, her eyes fixed at a point in the distance that seems to be just above my head, making her face as inscrutable as it always was—her high, elegant forehead, smooth and unlined, a billboard upon which nothing is written. Nor does she smile, which makes the clef in her chin more pronounced, her jawline softly squared above her slender neck. She sits perfectly erect without looking forced or uncomfortable. Perhaps she intended to look back on it years later and say, "That's where it began, my new life." I am struck with the thought that this is what she must have

meant to do: document herself as a woman come this far, the rest of her life ahead of her. (6)

Because of the nature of her mother's death and this last image left, Trethewey writes that she chose other stories to tell herself for years as she continues to see the portrait, adding, "the narrative of her making plans, stoically aware of what was to come, comforts me. I can't bear to think of the alternative, can't bear to think of her in that horrible moment, the sudden realization of her imminent death after allowing herself to believe she had escaped. Perhaps the truth lies somewhere between her hope and her pragmatism" (7). This space, between the hope of a different life and the pragmatism of trying to live the way one wants under threat of violence, marks the space in which so many Black girls and women live. Trethewey continues: "Hindsight makes me see the portrait differently now—how gloomy it is—as if the photographer meant to produce something artistic, rather than an ordinary studio portrait. It's as if he made of the negative space around her a frame to foreground some difficult knowledge: the dark past behind her, her face lit toward a future upon which her gaze is fixed" (7).

Beyond that: "And yet—undeniably—something else is there, elegiac even then: a strange corner of light just behind her head, perhaps the photographer's mistake, appearing as though a doorway has opened, a passage through which, turning, she might soon depart" (7). Between the photographer shooting her portrait and her narrative, Trethewey is able to see something different. "Looking at it now, with all I know of what was to come, I see what else the photographer has done. He's shot her like this: her black dress black as the scrim behind her so that, but for her face, she is in fact part of that darkness, emerging from it as from the depths of memory" (8).

Trethewey goes back to Atlanta nearly thirty years after her mother's death, specifically to the place where she cleaned her apartment at age nineteen, at which age she had to dispose of everything she could not carry with her— "all the furniture and household items, her clothing, her large collection of records" (disposed) and keeping "a few of her books, a heavy belt made of bullets, and a single plant she had loved—a dieffenbachia" (8). Trethewey writes: "Throughout my childhood it had been my responsibility to tend it, every week, dusting and misting the upper leaves and snipping the browned lower ones. *Be careful when you handle it*, my mother warned. A small precaution, seemingly unnecessary, but there is a toxin in the sap of the dieffenbachia; it oozes from the leaves and stems where they are cut. *Dumb cane*, the plant is called, because it can cause a temporary inability to speak. *Struck dumb*, we say when fear or shock or astonishment renders us mute; *dumb grief*, when the grief is not expressed in uttered words. I could not then grasp the inherent metaphor of the plant, my relationship with my mother, what it would mean that she had made its care my duty, while warning me of its danger" (9). She teaches her to care for what might disappear or even remove her abilities. The plant represents life, death, and even living silence if it is not cared for in the right way.

Through stories, through trauma, Trethewey offers the reader the gift of seeing both her and her mother's lives through her eyes: "What matters is the transformative power of metaphor and the stories we tell ourselves about the arc and meaning of our lives" (208). She also describes her own connected memories of driving past landmarks—the county courthouse where trials were held in 1985, the train station where her mother took the train downtown to work, the DeKalb County police station, the bypass loop around Metro Atlanta—and making her way down Memorial Drive, which "originates in the middle of the city . . . and winds east from downtown ending at Stone Mountain, the nation's largest monument to the Confederacy" (9). Trethewey writes, "To survive trauma, one must be able to tell a story about it" (208), as she describes the repeated dream of trying to save her mother before she wakes.

The dream, which she calls her "deepest wound" (210), comes to represent light for Trethewey:

> Something of the past was delivering to me again a familiar scene: that early image of my mother's face above me, eclipsing the sun, as I looked up at her from beneath the water's surface. Only now, it was in the negative— a reversal of light and dark that transformed her face into pure light ringed in darkness, the light all-consuming and piercing. (210)

As a responsible narrator even through her own trauma, Trethewey has to tell the reader that her stepfather, Joel Grimmette Jr., then Gwendolyn Grimmette's ex-husband, comes to Memorial Drive in Atlanta and takes her near the State car. She tries to reason with him, taking her things, and on his release he comes back again, blaming her. He stole a gun, and the record even records the wrong date, May 31, making "the date she died invisible in the document, takes five days from her, from me, as if they were irrelevant, as if it didn't matter, as if it were not important to be precise, to get it right" (189). This is after Joe shows up at Natasha's school during her senior year in high school, and she speaks, saying "Hey Joe" when he looked her way. This is after Natasha has written in a diary she knew he was reading, sure he would not tell her mother, "because that would mean he'd have to reveal what he was doing: invading the private world of the diary she had given me. I was also sure that he would never say anything to me about it, that he would rather pretend he'd never seen the words I had for him . . ." continuing, "I had begun to compose myself" (109).

Trethewey's metaphor of composition continues: "In the narrative of my life, which is the look backward rather than forward into the unknown and unstoried future, I emerged from the pool as from a baptismal font—changed, reborn—as if I had been shown what would be my calling even then. This is how the past fits into the narrative of our lives, gives meaning and purpose. Even my mother's death is redeemed in the story of my calling, made more meaningful rather than merely senseless. It is the story I tell myself to survive" (211). Her narrative of survival connects to Maya Angelou's "offering" in *Letter to My Daughter*:

> My life has been long, and believing that life loves the liver of it, I have dared to try many things, sometimes trembling, but daring, still. I have only included here events and lessons which I have found useful. I have not told how I have used the solutions, knowing that you are intelligent and creative and resourceful and you will use them as you see fit. (xi)

She includes "accounts growing up, unexpected emergencies, a few poems, some light stories to make you laugh and some to make you meditate" (xi) with advice. In addition to "never whine," she adds, "Be certain that you do not die without having done something wonderful for humanity" (xii).

Angelou grew up with her grandmother in Stamps, Arkansas, and was her "shadow" until she moved to San Francisco with her mother at thirteen:

> My grandmother didn't believe in hot-curling women's hair, so I had grown up with a braided natural. . . . I definitely did not belong. I walked around in that worldly atmosphere with my hands clasped behind my back, my hair pulled back in a tight braid, humming a Christian song.

My mother watched me for about two weeks. Then we had what was to become familiar as "a sit-down talk-to":

> She said, "Maya, you disapprove of me because I am not like your grandmother. That's true. I am not. But I am your mother and I am working

some part of my anatomy off to buy you good clothes and give you well-prepared food and keep this roof over your head. When you go to school, the teacher will smile at you and you will smile back. Other students you don't even know will smile and you will smile. But on the other hand, I am your mother. I tell you what I want you to do. If you can force one smile on your face for strangers, do it for me. I promise you I will appreciate it."

In these lessons, her mother taught her to be proud of herself. This pride carried into protection, as she is abused and kidnapped by a man simply known as Mark or "Two Finger Mark." After her mother's friend sees her and phones her mother, Angelou's mother looks for him in the bail bonds system. With Angelou hurt and unable to eat, and with a razor blade to her throat, Mark finally decides to go get her some juice to then "nurse [her] back to health." While he is gone, she writes:

> I knew where he had put the razor blade. If I could get it, at least I could take my own life and he would be prevented from gloating that he killed me.
>
> I began to pray.
>
> I passed in and out of prayer, in and out of consciousness, and then I heard shouting down the hall. I heard my mother's voice.
>
> Angelou continues recalling her mother's calls for help: "Break it down. Break the son of a bitch down. My baby's in there," adding, "Wood groaned then splintered and the door gave way and my little mother walked through the opening. She saw me and fainted. Later she told me that was the only time in her life she had done so," (32) and still later, Vivian Baxter, followed by three huge men into the room, was picked up and brought to the bed where she lay: "'Baby, baby. I'm so sorry.' Each time she touched me, I flinched. 'Call for an ambulance. I'll kill the bastard. I'm sorry . . .'" adding, "She felt guilty like all mothers who blamed themselves when terrible events happen to their children" (32), concluding, "I could not speak or even touch her but I have never loved her more than at that moment in that suffocating stinking room" (32).

Mark was found when two kids robbed a tobacco vendor's truck and threw the cartons into his car. When police arrested him, he called the same bail bondsman that Angelou's mother knew, who called her mother and gave the address. "Was that event incident, coincident, accident, or answered prayer?" (34) she asks, responding "I believe my prayers were answered" (34).

With messages to tell the truth and not to be vulgar, Angelou returns to stories of her mother, who picked up Angelou's son, Guy, twice a week and fed him, adding "I only went to her house at our appointed time. . . . She understood and encouraged my self-reliance" (52). As she visits one Red Rice Day, when her mother cooks a delicious dish for her, they leave the house together and walk through the streets of San Francisco.

"My mother stopped me and said, 'Baby . . . I've been thinking and now I am sure. You are the greatest woman I've ever met.'" (53). Angelou writes, "My mother was five feet four inches to my six-foot frame. I looked down at the pretty little woman, and her perfect makeup and diamond earrings, who owned a hotel and was admired by most people in San Francisco's black community." Her mother continued, "'You are very kind and very intelligent and those elements are not always found together. Mrs. Eleanor Roosevelt, Dr. Mary McLeod Bethune, and my mother—yes, you belong in that category. Here, give me a kiss'" (53).

Angelou's mother tells her she is not only great but the greatest, putting her name in line with other well known, distinguished, and yes, phenomenal women. The respect is also mutual, as Angelou adds:

> She kissed me on the lips and turned and jaywalked across the street to her beige and brown Pontiac. I pulled myself together and walked down to Fillmore Street. . . . My policy of independence would not allow me to accept money or even a ride from my mother, but I welcomed her wisdom. Now I thought of her statement. I thought, "Suppose she is right. She's very intelligent and she often said she didn't fear anyone enough to lies. Suppose I really am going to become somebody. Imagine." (54)

This imagining that she will "become somebody" helps to shape her mantra: "I decided the time had come when I should cut down on dangerous habits like smoking, drinking, and cursing. Imagine, I might really become somebody. Someday" (54).

Imagine

Angelou's imagination of a grander, beautiful life for herself extends to lessons about other cultures, such as in Morocco, where she learns that three to five raisins are put in a cup of coffee to show respect to visitors, stating, "I began this lifelong lesson. If human beings eat a thing, and if I am not so violently repelled by my own upbringing that I cannot speak, and if it is visually clean within reason, and if I am not allergic to the offering, I will sit at the table and with all the gusto I can manufacture I will join in the feast" (59), with this postscript: "I call this a lifelong lesson for I have not fully learned it and I am often put to the test and although I am no more or less squeamish than the next person, I have sometimes earned a flat 'F' at the test, failing miserably. But I get a passing grade more often than not. I just have to remember my grandmother and those four innocent raisins, which made me violently sick for one month" (60).

They extend to her decision to travel on a European tour as a principal dancer in *Porgy and Bess*, the George and Ira Gershwin opera, leaving Guy (then eight) with her mother and aunt. The company offered her money to send for Guy, but she writes that "there were already two children traveling with their parents, who exhibited behavior that I did not want my son to see, nor imitate" (63), so she stayed in hostels or with families to save money to send home to assuage the guilt. As she loses appetite, weight, and "interest in everything," Angelou just wanted to go home to her son. She sang in night-clubs and taught dance to pay her fare home and her replacement's fare to Europe. She writes:

"After nine days on the ship I arrived in New York and took a train for three days and nights to San Francisco. Our reunion was so emotional that I confess it may have sent me over the edge. I know I loved my son and I knew I was blessed that I was not in love with him, that I would not smother him by trying to be too close, and at the same time I would love him and raise him to be free and manly and happy as possible" (64). She then has a moment where she becomes anxious again, stating: "I realized it would be difficult if not impossible to raise a black boy to be happy and responsible and lib-erated in a racist society" (64). She thinks, "I could pick him up, open the window and jump" (64). Angelou goes to a psychiatric clinic, which nearly sends her away for having no appointment but then sends her to a young white doctor.

> I sat down and looked at him again and began to cry. How could this privileged young white man understand the heart of a black woman who was sick with guilt because she left her little black son for others to raise? Each time I looked up at him the tears flooded my face. Each time he asked what is the matter, how can I help you? I was maddened by the help-lessness of my situation. (65)

She then goes to her voice teacher and mentor, Frederick Wilkerson, who gives her scotch to put her to sleep. "Wilkie" tells her to write things she is grateful for. She writes: "I followed Wilkie's orders and when I reached the last line on the first page of the yellow pad, the agent of madness what routed" (66). Since, she wrote twenty-five books and "maybe fifty articles, poems, plays, and speeches" all with ballpoint pens and yellow pads (66). Her lesson:

"When I decide to write anything, I get caught up in my insecurity despite the prior accolades. I think, uh, uh, now they will know I am a charlatan that I really cannot write and write really well. I am almost undone, then I pull out a new yellow pad and as I approach the clean page, I think of how blessed I am" (66). In another powerful part of the text, Angelou reflects on what she thinks of her country, asking "Do I praise my country enough? Do I laud my fellow citizens enough?" (84). She discusses a number of people and lands on Fannie Lou Hamer:

Fannie Lou Hamer knew that she was one woman and only one woman. However, she knew she was an American, and as an American she had a light to shine on the darkness of racism. It was a little light, but she aimed it directly at the gloom of ignorance.

Fannie Lou Hamer's favorite was a simple song that we all know. We americans have sung it since childhood . . .

'This little light of mine,
I'm going to let it shine,
Let it shine,
Let it shine,
Let it shine.' (85)

Later, she speaks to the loss of her friends, James Baldwin; Alex Haley; Betty Shabazz; Ossie Davis; and Coretta Scott King, her "chosen sister" whose husband Martin was assassinated on her birthday and who shared calls, flowers, or cards for thirty years after his death.

Angelou writes:

When I find myself filling with rage over the loss of a beloved, I try as soon as possible to remember that my concerns and questions should be focused on what I learned or what I have yet to learn from my departed love. What legacy was left which can help me in the art of living a good life?

Did I learn to be kinder,
To be more patient,
And more generous,
More loving,

More ready to laugh,
And more easy to accept honest tears?
If I accept those legacies of my departed beloveds, I am able to say, Thank
You to them for their love and Thank You to God for their lives. (108)

We Are Still Here

A chapter of Angelou's book called "Condolences" simply states, "We are still here. Our hearts ache to support you. . . . We are always loving you. . . . You are not alone" (112). Her life lessons include choosing to return to the South to Wake Forest University for a job and for Americans showing ourselves "as courteous and courageous [and] well-meaning . . . Now" (126). Her narrative of the South continues:

They return to the South to find or make places for themselves in the land of their foreparents. They make friends under the shade of trees their ancestors left decades earlier. Many find themselves happy without being able to explain the emotion. I think it is simply that they feel generally important. . . . Even in little Stamps, Arkansas, black people walk with an air which implies "when I walk in they may like me or dislike me, but everybody knows I'm here." (131)

In the chapter "Surviving," she writes:

Where the winds of disappointment
Dash my dream house to the ground
And anger, octopus-like, wraps its tentacles around my soul
I just stop myself. I stop in my tracks
and look for one thing that can
heal me. . . . (135)

Angelou continues: "The second I realize I am gazing at a face/sweet with youth and innocents, I am drawn away/from gloom and despair, and into the pleasing climate/of hope" (136).

She extends the thread of hope in "Commencement Address," where she starts:

And now the work begins
And now the joy begins
Now the years of preparation
Of tedious study and

Exciting learning
are explained (145)

She continues: "For although you might all/Be bright, intellectually astute,/ You have had to use courage/To arrive at this moment" (146).

Between a Moan and a Lullaby

After discussing the poetry of Mari Evans, Sterling Brown, Claude McKay, Countee Cullen, and Langston Hughes, ending with Hughes's, "I, Too [Sing America]" (157), Angelou concludes with her grandmother's reminder of her power because of the word of God, which reminds Angelou that God exists. "I looked up to the sky and surely there, right there, between the sun and moon, stands my grandmother, singing a long meter hymn, a song somewhere between a moan and a lullaby and I know faith is the evidence of things unseen" (166).

Changing the Color of Celie's Blues

In *In Search of The Color Purple*, Salamishah Tillet writes (from an interview with Oprah Winfrey) that, after reading a review of *The Color Purple*, Oprah handed a copy of the book to every Black woman she knew and continues:

> When she left Baltimore to host *A.M. Chicago* in January 1984, she still carried *The Color Purple* in her backpack. On her walks from the studio to her home, she gave out books to strangers, even at nail and hair salons, even to women under the hair dryers. Of her instant attraction to Celie's story, she says, "I opened the page and saw *Dear God, fourteen years old, what's happening to me? Being a girl who at fourteen years old who had a baby.*" I was like, "There's another human being with my story" (130).

These stories moved, character by character, through generations as well, as Tillet writes of Oprah:

> [To] black girls of my generation, who watched Oprah from the comfort of our living rooms every day after school, she was more like our favorite aunt, the kind of woman we'd take advice from when our mothers were too strict or too uptight. (130)

Born to teenaged parents in Kosciusko, "one of the poorest and most segregated cities in Mississippi," Winfrey describes a story of repeated abuse and pregnancy after her mother left her behind when she moved to Milwaukee.

Abuse at the hands of relatives and men outside the family continued. Playing Sofia, however, offered multiple models of strong womanhood. Tillet writes: "Sofia's larger-than-life presence offers Celie a defiant model of black womanhood that she had never seen before--and neither had we on the American screen" (134). As Oprah continued to tell her story in her own studio and also "invited survivors of all ages and races in," Tillet writes that she "personalized her show to their experiences, and helped them break their own silence and end their lifelong shame," mixing "spirituality, self-help, and a concerted effort to believe sexual assault survivors" (139). This is the narrative that also affects Tillet as she tells her story of surviving sexual assault as a college student. Getting the opportunity to connect and share her narratives to those of Walker and Winfrey in the book offers a power of its own. The legacies of storytelling in the text extend from the narrative itself to the film, to the telling of impact on not only the author but also its most famous characters. Tillet adds: "'*The Color Purple* healed me,' Oprah says. 'Celie evolving and understanding her worth and her own beauty, her complete and total liberation by the end'" (138–39).

From being a teenage girl, fourteen years old and twice pregnant, with no one to tell her story to but God, to being the wife of a man who loves someone who becomes Celie's own lover and friend, to gaining a sisterly and even maternal relationship with Sofia, to finding and reconnecting with (and also writing to) her own biological sister, Nettie, Celie reveals her own light and legacies through Walker's narrative. From Alice Walker's narrative to the Broadway musical, to retelling and republication (and now an upcoming film), *The Color Purple* can never be looked at in the same way. Tillet concludes: "Oprah appeared before me as an impossibility, and in many ways, she was. Alice had Zora. Oprah had Alice. I had all of them" (143).

Recess
"Going Outside to Play"

In *Dressed In Dreams: A Black Girl's Love Letter to the Power of Fashion*, Tanisha Ford correlates attire with social relevance and mobility. Along with her own story of growing up in the Midwest, her hair, gang conflicts of the 1980s, and even decoration—airbrushing, rhinestones of the 1990s—Ford chronicles Black couture as well as the social and political relevance of Black women's dress. Along with her own narrative, Black girlhood narratives are also filled with stories of clothing as more than something to cover one's body.

My grandmother was always particular about our clothing (I am one of three girls who grew up in Georgia). Her name was Vanilla Bowman—her real name—and most people called her Van. She wasn't going most places without us dressed to the "nines," as children's dress goes. As young girls, this was usually pastel ruffle dresses; she particularly loved the ones with bells hidden under so that you jingled as you walked. There was something particular with her about taking out two or three brown-skinned girls, faces shining from leftover hair lotion or regular lotion, with white socks that folded over with ruffles and black patent leather shoes. People would usually remark about how "pretty" we were, and we would smile, for to be pretty was also to be seen and not heard.

Dress was a way to distinguish one's real or aspirational class and to distinguish one's behavior. "Good girls" dressed a certain way, not always as distinguished from an outside culture but internally as well. I see that this aesthetic still exists when I let my five-year-old, who has dressed herself for most of her life (because she, like most of us, is particular about how she feels in her clothes), walk down an aisle of a Black Presbyterian church in silver cowboy boots and a one-piece jumpsuit. Her excitement about wearing something she thought was cute matches how I felt when I used to get my hair pressed so it was just a little fluffy but still hung down and when I wore my first floral romper as well. My daughter decided during the COVID-19 pandemic to start her own business designing dresses for people who "dress like her" and to call it "Dreams and Dresses." Styles have changed through decades, but our culture as expressed in Black girls' attire has been around for years as well.

As I watch Megan Thee Stallion on *The Late Show with Stephen Colbert* (air date: December 9, 2020) discuss what is behind her "Bodyody" challenge, she states that the dance is just a way for her to stand in the mirror and appreciate her "fluff" after weight gained during the pandemic. She also, however, talks about being tall as a schoolgirl but having women tell her she was beautiful. She came to see her height as a reflection of her beauty, which connects to her image of herself today. Style, dance, music, performance, and art have also, for Black girls, been ways to play and to imagine their futures. When we change from dress clothes to "play clothes," magic is bound to occur. We move now to images and, finally, to futures of Black girlhood to imagine how we prepare to build.

Chapter 5

Build

From Black Girl Magic to Afrofutures

In 2018, Amy Sherald's painting *All Things Bright and Beautiful* (2016) was unveiled in Birmingham, Alabama, the site of the tragic deaths of four little Black girls killed in the bombing at the Sixteenth Street Baptist Church on September 15, 1963. Known for her official portrait of Michelle Obama painted for the Smithsonian Institution's National Portrait Gallery in 2017, Sherald uses the piece to represent Black girlhood with a girl in a flowered print dress looking ahead under a hand that shades her eyes. Hearkening to the idea of a future being bright, the image also suggests that protection is needed from the light as well. Of her work that features Black girlhood, Naima Green wrote in *The New York Times*, "The paintings demand that the viewers see the humanity on display. The subjects are real people, and they see us looking at them. It is impossible to look away" (https://www.artsbma.org/event/amy-sherald-in-conversation/). Sherald also created the image of Breonna Taylor in a beautiful teal dress for the cover of *Vanity Fair* in September 2020, named, simply, *Breonna Taylor: A Beautiful Life*.

The idea of what needs to happen to move successfully from Black girlhood to womanhood, a narrative of "becoming," connects to Michelle Obama's narrative of the same name, where she documents being a child in South Side Chicago from her birth in 1964 through first a successful career track of her own and then serving as the first lady to President Barack Obama in 2008. Put beside each other, along with Sherald's emergence from Georgia and Obama's from the South Side of Chicago, the narratives offer a framework of the path from Black girlhood to brilliant professional Black womanhood in its visual sense.

I saw the exhibition of her work, simply titled "Amy Sherald," in Spelman College's Art Museum in spring 2019, and as I walked around the campus where I taught in perhaps my most formative year as an academic (when I taught there full time as an instructor as I finished my dissertation), I also relished in the legacy of Black women writers I experienced as an emerging scholar there. From witnessing the work of Dr. Beverly Guy-Sheftall, the longtime director of the Women's Resource Center, to participating in the Annual Toni Cade Bambara Scholar-Activism Conference, to knowing that that was where many of my favorite writers began their careers, I thought of Spelman as a homeplace, as alumna Tayari Jones uses her homeplace of Atlanta to reminiscence on lost childhood in her novel *Leaving Atlanta* (based on the real childhood murders in Atlanta in my birth year of 1981, where I grew up just hours away, first in Columbus, Georgia, and then in Augusta, Georgia). Jones also delves into Black girlhood with a tale of sisters—a favored child born to married parents and another seeking claim to the name and birthright of her father in *Silver Sparrow*. These visual and literary texts with both connected and disparate narratives remind us of place, where we seek to be, and where we belong.

These representations of existence across media bring us to the present, where Beyoncé's 2020 visual album *Black Is King*, featuring her own daughter, Blue Ivy, and a presentation of her song "Brown Skin Girl" connect the joy of childhood to journeys through womanhood. Along with the significance of imagination, Black childhood and play reveal joy and honesty in connection with narratives.

Toni Cade argues in her anthology *The Black Woman* that "What typifies the current spirit is an embrace, and embrace of the community and a hardheaded attempt to get basic with each other" (1). I argue that the communal spirit represented in this work becomes the model for the many texts that come to represent Black girlhood from the 1970s through the present. In Eleanor Traylor's introduction to the text, she cites "At millennium 147 studies of that life and work have been produced by readers who love conversations with Toni Cade Bambara. . . . Of these, 28 have targeted *The Black Woman: An Anthology* as founding text of a 'womanist' evolutionary enunciation'" (x). Traylor continues, "not only did *The Black Woman* launch a face, it unveiled and named a landscape as resplendent as the world of literature offers," citing Toni Morrison's *The Bluest Eye* and Alice Walker's *The Third Life of Grange Copeland*, both published in the same year as *The Black Woman* in 1970, as "commanders in the field of fiction" (xi).

Other texts from that "year of wonders" that Traylor cites included Maya Angelou's *I Know Why the Caged Bird Sings* as "progenitor of the contemporary life narrative," as well as *Family Pictures* and *Riot* by Gwendolyn Brooks, Margaret Walker's *Prophets for a New Day*, Audre Lorde's *Cables to Rage*,

Sonia Sanchez's *We a Baddddd People*, and Mari Evans' *I Am a Black Woman* (xi). Across genres, through poetry, essays, and memoirs, Traylor cites an "Afrafemme" worldview that these texts represent in conversation with each other. Nikki Giovanni's "Woman Poem" and "Nikki-Rosa" and Audre Lorde's "Naturally" and "And What About the Children," among others, represent a worldview that begins with youth as well.

Traylor argues: "*The Black Woman: An Anthology* erases mule-minded boundaries as between orality and the written word, beautiful writing and investigative prose, professional writers and newly awakened rising voices, man and woman at the level of awakening self-discovery" (xv). I also argue that these texts contribute to a conversation about young adulthood that continues to grow in volumes published in the following years, including, as Traylor cites, Toni Cade Bambara's *Tales and Stories for Black Folks* (1971), *The Salt Eaters* (1980), and *Those Bones Are Not My Child* (published posthumously in 2000). But she also continues to gather the works of others, including students in the Fort Greene Young Writer's Project in Brooklyn and "'the Newark Mamas—mothers back in school, working for their college degrees at Livingston College, Rutgers University' (1) where she taught" (xv). This is her continuing of her legacy with those who are living and working in community.

Traylor also cites the voice of Farah Jasmine Griffin (most recently, the author of *Read Until You Understand*) seeing the text at "'seven or eight years old' . . . at Robins Bookstore in Philadelphia" (x) and stating: "'In the still color-conscious black world of McDaniel Elementary School in South Philadelphia, I was constantly reminded that I was 'black' (which always seemed to be qualified by phrases such as 'and ugly,' 'and shiny,' 'and crispy'). . . . I was in desperate need of a browner, Afroed revolutionary image" (on x). The narrative excerpt concludes, "By possessing the book, I could possess the woman, could become the woman—or so I reasoned" (Glaude 113–14, in Cade Bambara, x).[1]

In addition to the "narratological practice" of gathering ("work[ing] to recommend to ever-new reading audiences the absolute necessity and the joy of *gathering* together to think deeply and act decisively in behalf of 'salvation'—another of her most frequently used words" (xvii), "womanword:

---

1. Griffin, Farah Jasmine. "Conflict and Chorus: Reconsidering Toni Cade's *The Black Woman: An Anthology*," in *Is It Nation Time? Contemporary Essays on Black Power and Black Nationalism*, ed. Eddie S. Glaude Jr. (Chicago: University of Chicago Press, 2002).

an eye-to-eye, word-to-word encounter in which language explores itself as talking-text-in-writing" also becomes the woman*work* of bringing Black girls into the circles of knowledge. As Traylor notes: "womanword is also Toniword is blackwomanword everywhere alive in the universe of word that talks and writes better than it has been trained" (xvii).

As Toni Cade Bambara asks, "Who is the Black Woman?" noting that "she is a college graduate. A *drop-out*. A student. *A wife*. A divorcee. *A mother*. A lover. *A child of the ghetto*. A product of the bourgeoisie. *A professional writer*. A person who never dreamed of publication . . ." (Cade, First Edition, cited, xviii). Traylor also notes that she is a "must-read text to be delivered into the hands of all of us who work to achieve the wonderful light of knowledge, love, and beauty . . . and everlasting *yes*" (xviii). I also argue that Black women writers have made Black girls "an everlasting yes"—yes to celebrating themselves and ourselves. Yes to acknowledging trauma and pain but also power. And yes to showing themselves honestly and truly in many forms.

Black girls have also been shifting and adjusting however they can. Alice Childress's narrator Rainbow Jordan in a book of the same name (1982) notes: "There's school. They lookin for a parent to show. I've hollered 'She's sick' so many times till I can't pull that one again. My soul is hurtin" (7). Rainbow's mother is in and out of her life, and her father is also inconsistent, but research on her people motivates her:

> One paper I once got a B-plus was "Accomplishments of Black people in America"—I got the bonus for research. Wrote a gallopin paper because I found lots of books on accomplishments. I told how Benjamin Banneker was a good scientist and also help lay out the plan for Washington, D.C. Told bout George Washington Carver and discoveries he made to put the peanut to use; made oil, face powder and gangs of other products. He discovered the same for the sweet potato . . . and *gave* it all to America. (7–8)

She adds: "I also got me a B on a paper bout 'The Black Family'—I told bout Martin Luther King, Jr., and his wife and children, bout Medgar Evers and a boss line-a beautiful Black families. . . . Now, I'm standin here and nobody to talk to but me, myself and I. Black ball players and movie stars just truly fine . . . but they can't pay our rent. We gotta find some money. That's all my mother is away trying to do—find us some money" (8). Her family structure is what challenges her to look at other narratives to find a sense of support. Although they aren't traditional parents, she has "people" and a foster family for when additional help is needed.

Rainbow says: "I never really had a *mama* and a *daddy*. I got a Kathie and a Leroy. He'd come see us off and on. I like Leroy very much and remember him. I liked him every time I saw him. He has a nice face" (9). She also focuses on positives: her name, at least as her mother says it, and her village. "Kathie picked my name, 'Rainbow.' She say it sound like pretty colors and also people tell how there's a pot-a gold at the end." Kathie works as a go-go dancer, on top of Aid to Dependent Children check, but there is not always money to go around (9). Rainbow states: "Round our neighborhood, I got to know all the ladies who take care of children while the mothers go off to work. I fast changed from one to another cause we'd fall behind in payment and not catch up. Kathie smile pretty and laugh so fine till people always carry her tab longer than most. But, after all, they can't do it forever" (9). She also suffers from her mother's physical assaults, noting: "I know how to back off and keep my distance. One time, when I was little, she hit me so hard till I got a black-and-blue on my arm and shoulder. Just pounded on me and mad as the devil. Well, I had done wrong. Drank milk from the container without askin. She had plans for us to use that milk next day" (10).

When Kathie threatens to beat Rainbow, she locks herself in the bathroom and looks on the bright side with what she receives out of her mother's guilt: "Next day was like nothin happen. Kathie kissin me, bakin a cake and makin me eat nearly all of it. When the A.D.C. check came she bought me pair-a black patent-leather sandals with matchin shoulder-strap bag. Some of the best presents I ever got was the day after a beatin" (11). During the story, she is proud because her mother took up for her but is now waiting on casework: "I rather be stayin with my own mother in our apartment, no matter how perfect anybody else might be. Truth be told, I *can't* stay with her if she drops out and nobody knows where she's at. I could stay and take care-a myself, like I do when she's home, but fourteen is call 'minor.' So whatcha gonna do?" (11).

The exchange between foster mother Josephine and Kathie after Kathie explains being away shows Josephine's concerns with Kathie's behavior and resentment that Rainbow always wants to return to her mother: "What was the delay? Another man in a scroungy hotel room? Mean thought. I'm jealous. The girl is always glad to go back, no matter what. I give the best of myself . . . and she's ever ready to leave" (14). When Josephine's husband, Hal, teases about Rainbow being the child to brighten up Christmas at fourteen, she reflects: "I tried to make light of his remark about the girl. I resented him taking out feelings about me on someone else. 'She has never been able to be a child . . . according to her caseworker. Let's make a nice holiday for her'" (16). As a part of Rainbow's village, Josephine tries to give her the space to be a child even when the world does not see her as such.

In Sapphire's *Push* (1996), the "I was born" narrative of the nineteenth-century narratives of enslavement (and documentation of existence) is replaced with a different beginning, "I was left back" (3), as protagonist Claireece "Precious" Jones narrates, "I was left back when I was twelve because I had a baby for my fahver. That was in 1983. I was out of school for a year. This gonna be my second baby" (3). The book begins with Precious's complete understanding of why she has been retained in school and also of her current condition. She also, however, understands how her children are situated in relation to her academic standing. Precious continues, "My daughter got Down Sinder. She's retarded. I had got left back in the second grade too, when I was seven, 'cause I couldn't read (and I still peed on myself). I should be in the eleventh grade, getting ready to go into the twelf' grade so I can gone 'n graduate. But I'm not. I'm in the ninfe grade" (3). She is clear that she is not the typical high schooler or even the typical parent, and she expresses her injustice with assessment of the circumstances. "I got suspended from school 'cause I'm pregnant which I don't think is fair. I ain' did nothin'!" (3). And all of this, her condition, is expressed before we see her name.

The narration of Precious's name itself becomes part of the story and also a reason for not sharing too much: "My name is Claireece Precious Jones. I don't know why I'm telling you that. Guess 'cause I don't know how far I'm gonna go with this story, or whether it's even a story or why I'm talkin; whether I'm gonna start from the beginning or right from here or two weeks from now" (3). She continues, "Sure you can do anything when you talking or writing, it's not like living when you can only do what you doing. Some people tell a story 'n it don't make no sense or be true. But I'm gonna try to make sense and tell the truth, else what's the fucking use? Ain' enough lies and shit out there already?" (3–4). Without overtheorizing Precious's telling her life story (or Sapphire using the lens of a girl who has been left behind in a number of ways), it is important to look at the first-person voice and the agency of her character to refute the "lies and shit" by speaking for herself. With her ability to say what she sees and why she responds to those who try to make her feel stupid, Precious holds on to what power she has, even in circumstances of powerlessness.

When the math teacher demands that she turns to a certain page, Precious responds, "Mutherfucker I ain't deaf" (4) and then asserts her right to learn when ordered to leave the room, "I ain' going nowhere mutherfucker till the bell ring. I came here to learn maff and you gon' teach me," (5) but she continues, "I didn't want to hurt him or embarrass him like that you know. But I couldn't let him, anybody, know, page 122 look like page 152, 22, 3, 6, 5—all the pages look alike to me. 'N I really do want to learn" (5). Through this lens, the reader can focus less on Precious's behavior and more on the reasons why she is outside the system of educational justice. She, and we, understand what is fundamentally unfair about the ways she has been treated. "I'm gonna break through or somebody gonna break through to me—I'm gonna learn, catch up, be normal, change my seat to the front of the class" (5). Through the book, we hope for Precious to move to the front, which she does, in a different way through the literacy course and GED program.

Ms. Rain, Precious's teacher, encourages her to write and to tell her story, and Precious responds to the motivation through the story. "Ms Rain say more now, much more. She wan more from me" (98). Ms Rain tells her to walk with the journal. "Everywhere you go . . . journal go," and Precious follows suit. "You know I go walk with Abdul etc., take journal, write stuff in journal. Learnin lot: to too two. Three different 2 words. . . . Four for fore. Three four words" (98). Literacy becomes the journey that Precious takes us on along with her. In reading the journal, we see her assessment of herself and where she wants to go. "Ms Rain tell to <u>koncentrate</u> on my story. When I . . . can not speall a word Ms. Rain tell me sound out firs lettr c_____ and draw a lin. Thas concentrate. Latrer she will fill in rite spelling for me. But my spelling is impruv. Way way improve" (98). Most significant, however, is that she learns to name her pain, words for mental health, for example. "Ms Rain say I seem dpress. depres<u>sion</u> is she say ang<u>er</u> turn in" (98). Without these words, without the acknowledgment of the complicated things she is experiencing, she cannot fully tell her story.

Words give shape to experiences and help her determine who she will continue to become. "For/a monf it bin like this. I feel daze./Ms Rain see it/say you not same girl I kno./is tru. I am a difrent/person/anybuddy wood be don't u think?/don't/u/think" (99). In circumstances similar to Pecola's, Precious is able to emerge with the support of her community and succeed in her own way. The text ends with a poem called "Untitled" in Precious's words: "I can see/I can read/nobody can see now/but I might be a poet, rapper, I got/water colors/my child is smart/my CHILDREN/is alive"; it goes on to say: "PLAY THE HAND YOU GOT/housemother say./HOLD FAST TO DREAMS/Langston say./GET UP OFF YOUR KNEES/Farrakhan say./CHANGE/Alice Walker/say." (unpaginated). The citation does not go unnoticed, as I think of the trope of searching for the maternal and matriarchal guidance that Walker pursues in *In Search of Our Mothers' Gardens*; Precious chooses what she wants from all of these voices but decides, in the line of Black foremothers, to change.

I add to these narratives the story of the sister protagonists from Netflix's *Sisters on Track*, who were named junior Olympians and ran for the Jeuness Track Club in Brooklyn while living in New York without a permanent home until filmmaker and producer Tyler Perry found and funded an apartment for them. The girls, Tai, Rainn, and Brooke Sheppard, ages nine, eleven, and twelve at the time of filming in 2017, want to be a math teacher, lawyer, and judge. Tai dreams of becoming an Olympian and also a biochemist. Brooke states, "I . . . want to be an artist and track runner. Both." Their Mom, Tonia Handy, states: "They have hopes," despite Brooke's admission, "In the shelter I thought it was all over, I thought we were going to be homeless for the rest of our lives. . . . I would just think about what might happen if the rest of my life was like this."

Brooke's musing references a thought process that has always been, to show the ways in which this freedom has been and can be realized. I find, as a centerpiece, that I come back to the narratives of four little girls, four little Black girls, as a requiem. (Requiem: mass for the repose of the souls of the dead, an act or token of remembrance.) I locate the uses of memoir fiction as a way to think about the dead (or, in this case, hopeless spirits) moving through spaces.

Girlhood remembrance involves dramatizing and documenting their experiences. How do Black girls move beyond restrictive spaces, then, to find the freedom of their dreams?

We can trace this freedom through narratives of space travel in, for instance, *Mae Among the Stars* and *Hidden Figures*, where the stories of Mae Jemison and Katherine Johnson, among others, are told. But we can find the roots of these narratives in Phillis Wheatley's imagining herself being brought "from Africa to America" so that she may tell her own story in her way, the story of an Ethiop, to which she refers to herself, finding and sharing a sense of self and identity. We find roots of Afrofuturism in Douglass's use of Sandy's root to beat his overseer enough to know that he was a force to be reckoned with.

We find Harriet Jacobs's narrative of play as one of pain, as she is not allowed to join with her mother as she becomes a servant to her master's household, and later, the purpose of hiding isn't to be sought. I place the narratives of Afrofuturism that we find in children's literature then in categories similar to that of adult literature. Narratives of enslavement are magical realism—stories of escape but also stories of character and triumph. These narratives also include biographical lives—important figures, sometimes gifted with extraordinary characteristics, and narratives of the future, space, and beyond. When we return to 1964 and 1965, after the Civil Rights Acts, where federal funding was poured into the publication of texts that were not necessarily positive representations of Black childhood, we can ask, When do we get to the future?

Narratives of return include *The People Could Fly* (1985) by Virginia Hamilton, narratives of the 1980s, neoslave narratives imagining endings that are different from just death (although death can be imagined as a type of freedom in itself). The conclusion, "Building the Worlds of Our Dreams," imagines a different ending to stories we hear far too often. It is *Sesame Street* of 1969–2019, imagining that kids in urban spaces could move through their imaginations, *Reading Rainbow* encouraging us to "take a look, it's in a book" in the 1980s and 1990s. It is using the eyes of a child to see a bigger world.

Black Girl, Southern, Spring/Summer 2021

We begin again, with the return to nonnormalcy that demands the time, labor, and energy of Black women and girls across the nation and world. In the southern United States, it seems as if that ticking clock—go, do, be— never really stopped. Thrust into the pandemic in March 2020, we were also frozen in space to watch, witness, and experience the tragic deaths of our kin and those who could have been.

As a Blackgirl student at Duke University (in that order), I remember watching the film *Girl, Interrupted* in one of my favorite Women's Studies courses on womanhood, girlhood, and trauma. Although I don't remember the details of the film and perhaps have even blocked them out, I recall feeling like a witness to white girlhood and adolescence unraveling (or even already unraveled). I remained approximate to the dysfunction that didn't feel like my own yet from which I could not disconnect.

Like many other Black girls, southern, and likely internationally, I remember striving to succeed, to make my parents and family proud when, as a parent of four young children under eleven and experiencing the grief of losing her younger sister, resting may have been all my mother could do to keep us alive. I remember going through periods of not talking to my mother, spending periods reading books and communicating only through writing to gain additional attention (although I was highly respectful most of the time at school and elsewhere).

But I was also the child of a visible middle-class professional family with privileges that allowed us to navigate between private and public schools, a distinguished Black church in a smaller southern city, and social organizations that gave us access to whatever we wanted or needed and that resulted in educational and professional opportunities whether we chose to take advantage or not. Being a Southern Black girl—or Blackgirl, Southern—was and is a many vexed and complicated positionality, as striving for success became a way to also make oneself relevant in society. The motto was to make oneself useful, and so the idea of "use" later grew into more harmful substances to other members of my family and community. I was addicted to being helpful and smart; although genuine, it never suggested other ways to actually be.

And so, decades later, this book discusses, reveals, and uncovers the legacies of Southern girlhood and activism that trace being and doing as a way of life for Black girls in particular. Less research and more explication (expansion) of existence, this book will trace stories of Black Southern girlhood and the places and spaces in which we move.

I could not have finished this book before 2021, and it seems like it took forever because, in March 2020, the world seemed to fall apart with a global pandemic that no one seemed to see or want to see. What seemed like "other people's problems"—and, to be real, a skepticism and privilege rooted in xenophobia and lack of concern for what does not affect us—quickly shifted us to our homes, some for close to or even over a year, without the privileges of service (and, honestly, of care and concern) that we were used to from others. Questions ranged from "Who will watch/teach/cook for us and our children?" to "Who will care for our elders?" to "How will we see each other?" to "What will we do without physical and even emotional contact?"

During this period, my family was both a haven and a source of concern, especially my daughter who aged from six to eight during the pandemic and was interrupted at a key point in the development of friendships and social engagement in general. Although my mother never said this to me, the line, "I am not one of your little friends" often resonated, as I realized that I was a source of human existence and acknowledgment for her in a way that did not affect my older child, who was already part of gaming and online communities.

"Who is going to play with me?" she often asked, as I became the person who went outside for hopscotch or kickball, or to draw with chalk on the sidewalk. The amusement of being best friends may have worn off for her before it did for me. I was generally glad to be reminded to play, even at times that previously would have seemed inopportune. I would say "Sorry, I can't meet at that time. I need to play with my daughter," and even after the children went back to school, I would try to cut off any dialogues by three or four o'clock to share afternoon time. The whole game changed because of the pandemic, and not only for the worst. Why did it take the world shutting down for us to connect, to value each other, and to care about what we were going through?

Play as Past and Present: Aesthetics and Empowerment in Black Girlhood Literature

As a young girl raised in the South, I spent much of summer daylight hours outside, but playing outdoors came at the cost of extensive cleaning rituals at the end of each day. Baths were where we were instructed to touch every part of our bodies, as my grandmother said to get all of the places touched and untouched by the outdoor sun. When old enough to be left unsupervised, bathtime for Black children can also become playtime. Unlike showers, where the water is running and can be mandated not to be "wasted," bath water was good until it got cold. For me, that water meant time to play freely, to travel to places where there is nowhere else to be.

Bathtime was my grandmother's freedom from work in an unrelenting sun and, back then, what she could provide for her grandchildren after a day of play in her own beautiful home. This home was different from the one where she grew up, where her sharecropping family used baths practically, to wash off the work of the day. Baths weren't places of everyday joy. To use them excessively was wasteful. Because of her labor and the labor of my parents, baths represented joy, connection with self, and a space away from the outside world. They represented resistance to spaces where Black girlhood was public and could be disciplined and regulated. Baths, although often short in houses full of people, allowed me time and space to dream and imagine what my girlhood could be.

Even with the positive and pleasant memories that evoke girlhood for me, I cannot separate them from the traumas of those who came before me and what Shange describes in *for colored girls* as "shattered pieces . . . of never having been a girl." I end as I began, with several questions. First, how do literary narratives construct memories by and about African American girls? Where do our memories come from? Who tells the stories? As Jacqueline Woodson represents in *Brown Girl Dreaming*, dreams are also ways in which Black girls move away from visions of Black girlhood that have been created for them and toward transformative justice, through dreams of freedom and imagining different pathways.

They are narratives that can be found in stories told to children but that resist the boundaries of "simple" childhood. They are stories that move us from southern to northern spaces and even to outer space. They are stories that transcend history and move through generations.

Black children—and, inherently, Black girls—dream of different ways of being, of existing, and these dreams are represented in a literary canon of Black women writers. There are Isie Watts and Janie Crawford of Zora Neale Hurston's imagination, who want to travel the world and escape the bounds of girlhood and domesticity. There is Toni Morrison's Nel Wright, who sees a future beyond her mother's domination, and Pecola Breedlove, whose eyes finally become blue enough (if only in her own mind) to escape what she has seen. There is Sapphire's Claireece "Precious" Jones, who dreams of herself as more than an illiterate teenage mother and incest victim. Other little girls are made of "sugar and spice and everything nice." Black girls, however, can contain dark secrets. They are expected to grow into roles of parent and caregiver beyond their childhood too fast. There is no surprise when they do. They are lost and unwanted, trapped in systems of social welfare and foster care. But they are also representatives of Afrofuturistic visions of Black girlhood, of the "quare" routes and pathways of existence.

These pathways are invoked by Ntozake Shange imploring, "somebody, anybody, [to] sing a black girl's song," to "bring her out/to know herself/to know you . . . she's been dead so long/closed in silence so long/she doesn't know the sound/of her own voice/her infinite beauty" (4). They are shaped in Nikki Giovanni's poetic representations in *Spin a Soft Black Song* of shared "desire to plant a masthead for doves . . . To spin a soft Black song . . . To waltz with the children . . . To the mountains of our dreams" (vi). In these stories, poems, and narrative spaces, imagined dreams of black girlhood are realized.

Giovanni wrote for "yvonne," who "stood there unsmiling/with collard greens/and sensible shoes/on her way to becoming a good Black woman," but she also wrote "barbara poems," that "are round/and soft/with explosives inside." Put together, these poems documented traditional pathways to grow into a "good Black woman" but also suggested that typical senses and sensibilities are not the only paths to finding one's way in the world. Shange's desire for a "black girl's song" becomes an imperative that Giovanni takes up, as she sings several songs of Black children, specifically Black girls. It is not just anyone who takes this initiative, but a poet who remembers her own Black girl dreams from Knoxville, Tennessee, which Giovanni covers in "Knoxville," as she details the time she spent with her grandmother in the mountains making ice cream, to the eyes through which she sees the worlds of others.

Black girls dreaming becomes a trope especially in twentieth-century literature, and this book only discusses some of the many examples of Black girlhood that emerge in narratives of Black women's empowerment from the late nineteenth century to the present. What is significant is the ways in which these stories connect Blackness to the quareness of girlhood. Black girlhood and its power to imagine and to celebrate what is and what is to become is already quare in the imagination of a life beyond the ordinary. Through these stories, I discuss the pathways and physical spaces that represent Black girl quareness and authors who "sing a black girl's song" so that their voices are heard.

To quote Charlene Carruthers in *Unapologetic: A Black, Queer, and Feminist Mandate for Radical Movements*, these voices are heard as we write and think about "Black radical, feminist, queer, and anti-capitalist theories and practices" (ix) for and about Black youths. These readings uncover our potential to move from radical and even ordinary visions of Black girlhood (including the ability to dream) toward freedom and justice. The texts in this essay (and many that are not mentioned) allow Black girl characters and their readers to dream of different places and ways of being while understanding the reality of what it means to exist where we are.

Echoing Isie Watts's wish to simply go up the road to Orlando in 1920s rural Florida in Zora Neale Hurston's "Drenched in Light" are enduring narratives and recent retellings of girls and women migrating to other cities "and beyond." Desires and demands for education and mobility (both social and physical) that were thought of as "queer" in early narratives of the twentieth century became necessary for national progress in arguments for civil rights. Margot Lee Shetterly's best-selling *Hidden Figures* and its concurrently published Young Readers' Edition (2016) chronicle the experiences of African American women Katherine Johnson (mathematician), Dorothy Vaughan (supervisor and mathematician), and Mary Jackson (who sued to gain entrance to night school to become an engineer), who assisted in the efforts of the National Aeronautics and Space Administration, or NASA, to launch its first space missions from the Langley Research Center in Virginia from 1958 to 1963. Dreams to go to outer space were not yet real for these women, but they were depended on as essential in advancing the United States's race to keep up with the then-Soviet Union's 1957 launch of Sputnik 1. Arguments in these texts for the rights of Black women, whose ideas for their own incredible narratives began as early as childhood, span across southern and northern spaces, including segregated Hampton, Virginia, where the "hidden figures'" stories begin.

However, as Shetterly argues, everyone knew the stories of African American involvement and employment at Langley (i.e., the figures were only "hidden" to outsiders). I posit that this is also a metaphor for quare Black southern girlhood. It is a given that Black girls have dreams and desires that cannot be stifled simply by telling them what they cannot do, including defining their social positions and relationships. Shetterly emphasizes that the stories of Black women's capabilities within the realm of science, thought strange or unprecedented by outsiders, were well known within the Black communities where Langley was located. Although Black women as scientists in the 1950s and 1960s may seem a queer notion today, these women's quare dreams to help the United States get to outer space were not.

Stories of Black women's aspirations from childhoods (extending beyond what those within and outside their communities can imagine for them) are told by and for all ages, including the very young. The Langley story is retold by Shetterly for an even younger audience in her recent picture book, *Hidden Figures: The True Story of Four Black Women and the Space Race* (2018), and the narrative of migrations beyond even our planet is told and retold in narratives about the first Black woman astronaut, Mae Jemison. Children's stories like *Mae Among the Stars* (2018) detail for four- to eight-year-olds the narrative of "Little Mae" as a dreamer. Roda Ahmed writes: "They say that daydreamers never succeed, but little Mae was different" (3). Mae wants to see Earth, as she tells her parents (who support her dream). She reads about astronauts and makes her own costume, even though her teacher tells her the best she can aspire to be is a nurse. Ahmed writes, "Mae went on dreaming, believing, and working really hard. And guess what—She went to space and waved to her mom and dad on Earth." Ahmed concludes with the real-life story of Dr. Mae Carol Jemison, who was born in 1956 in Decatur, Alabama, and always had a love for science before going on to enroll at Stanford University at the age of sixteen and earning her doctorate in medicine from Cornell Medical College. Jemison was accepted into NASA's astronaut training program and became the first African American female astronaut and the first African American woman in space.

What we now know as Afrofuturistic representations of girlhood are evident in the nineteenth-century nonfiction narratives, as Harriet Jacobs,

Harriet Tubman, and others designed individual and collective journeys to freedom. After bearing two children fathered by a white politician—and finding that their births did not, as she had she expected, bring her and her children freedom from a predatory master and jealous mistress—Jacobs escaped to a garret in her grandmother's attic in Edenton, North Carolina, where she remained for seven years, subject to seasonal elements, vermin, and a paralyzing lack of physical movement. Painful representations of what Jacobs's family suffered and the emotional and physical violence committed by the Norcom family who enslaved her make the horrific events and the audacity of the freedom dreams she depicts in *Incidents in the Life of a Slave Girl* seem incredible. Indeed, Jacobs's book (published under the pseudonym Linda Brent) was read as fiction until research by Jean Fagan Yellin definitively established the veracity of Jacobs's story and authorship.

Jacobs's story begins in childhood, watching her mother serve her own white sister until her early death, seeing her brother not be able to go to their father when also called by their master, and becoming subject to her master's advances before reaching adolescence. One might argue (and arguments have been made) that she had to adopt her own notions of freedom to substitute for the lack of consent that she actually had in her life. A quare framework helps us to understand better both Jacobs's negotiations of her sexuality and the resistance she encounters from white and Black adults. Quare notions come to represent the plan to arrange her own path to freedom (which her grandmother opposed, ripping away her mother's wedding ring when Jacobs confesses her first pregnancy) and to endure the time spent enclosed in a space in which she could not even stand (but which she imagined and knew would be better than the experience of enslavement from which she came).

Contemporary retellings of journeys that began as dreams of freedom have been carried through narratives, specifically about children and, more specifically, Black girls as well. Stories of travel that allow these girls to leave fixed identities and even time periods include Faith Ringgold's *Aunt Harriet's Underground Railroad in the Sky* (1992), which she dedicates to her great-great-great-grandmother Susie Shannon, who "survived very difficult times so that [Ringgold] could be free." Alongside such retellings of oral narratives such as *The People Could Fly* (by Virginia Hamilton), which tells the story of enslaved people rising up and taking to the sky, Faith Ringgold's *Aunt Harriet's Underground Railroad in the Sky* tells the story of a girl, Cassie, and her baby brother, Be Be, "flying among the stars, way way up, so far up the mountains looked like pieces of rock candy and the oceans like tiny cups of tea" (1). They find an "old ramshackled train in the sky" and a tiny woman in a conductor's uniform announcing the schedule to "Maryland, Delaware, Pennsylvania, New Jersey, New York, Niagara Falls, Canada" (2). The narrator describes the "hundreds of bedraggled men, women and children [who] filled the sky and boarded the dusty old wooden train" like "watching a silent movie." (2). And as a quare Black girl is prone to do, Cassie leaves her prescribed space, first following her brother Be Be who gets onto the train, then seeing through the clouds a message, through the clouds to "Go free North or Die!"—a message to which she seeks to adhere.

As Cassie tries to navigate this journey, she hears the voice of Harriet Tubman, "Aunt Harriet," who teaches her about the passengers being brought from Africa, many dying on ships, those who survived being subject to violence and/or being sold. Cassie learns about how enslaved Black couples had to "jump the broom" because they were not permitted to marry legally; how it was against the law to learn to read or write, meet, or preach. Aunt Harriet tells Cassie to "follow the North Star," with instructions to find Underground Railroad agents for lodging, clean clothes, and food, adding, "But until you reach Canada, you are not safe. Go and don't turn back" (11).

Following her own journey from a childhood and adulthood in the institution of slavery, Aunt Harriet becomes a model for a young girl's freedom as well. The metaphor of the "railroad," physical pathways through thousands of miles and a number of states, becomes a futuristic vision of faster mobility that also halts time, as it only follows the same route every one hundred years. Aunt Harriet states, "Sometimes the train is a farmer's wagon. Sometimes it is a hearse covered with flowers—inside, a live slave hides in a coffin. You missed this train, Cassie. But you can follow, always one stop behind" (11). Cassie has the benefit of being able to fly (a nod to her ancestors who took to the sky). But Aunt Harriet warns: "though you can fly, being a slave will suck you to the ground like quicksand. You will have to walk many miles through the woods and waters on blistered feet" (11). In its retelling of a freedom narrative, this story connects past desires for and designs of collective freedom and present/future needs to know that history to gain new understandings of freedom.

Like Aunt Harriet's real-life narrative, Cassie's story also ends in freedom, where she is reunited with her brother, Be Be, who has a real live Baby Freedom tied to his back. The celebration of the reunion culminates in a big feast in honor of the one-hundredth anniversary of Harriet Tubman's first flight to freedom in 1849: and for Aunt Harriet "for taking us from slavery to freedom and for being the Moses of her people" (25). Knowing that a world could and would be better was the drive for Harriet Tubman and the passengers on the Underground Railroad, and it was the connection of the children, like the author herself, to their great-great-grandparents.

As this book begins, quare journeys, including those that are foundational in Black girlhood, inspire quare narratives of freedom written by Black women authors. These narratives cover a wide span of time from the nineteenth century (and even earlier, if we imagine original narratives thought of, if not written, by Black girls in the South from the circumstances of their enslaved childhoods). They are told in stories such as *The Patchwork Quilt*, by Valerie Flournoy, in which a young girl, Tanya, connects with her grandmother while making a patchwork quilt from scraps of worn clothing and material. "Sometimes the old ways are forgotten" (3), Grandma says as she tries to explain the significance of making and keeping old quilts. Like quilts, stories are the ways of passing on individual efforts toward freedom and mobility. Tanya has to wait an entire year as she and Grandma collect pieces for the quilt.

Through Halloween and Christmas, and through Grandma's illness when she closes her tired eyes, leaving the family to work on the quilt, Tanya stops working when she feels someone (Grandma) is missing from the quilt. Tanya removes a few squares from Grandma's old quilt and adds them to theirs, which magically gives Grandma new life. She is able to add the last row of patches, dedicated to Tanya from her "Mama and Grandma." The end of this story is not only representative of Black women's narratives of resilience but also a reminder that a story is not over until it is passed on (to recall a phrase from Toni Morrison's *Beloved*, in which telling stories also prevents repeating a painful history of enslavement and infanticide).

Narratives of Black girlhood also expand historical narratives for more contemporary audiences, as Margaree King Mitchell writes in *Granddaddy's Gift* (1997), about a girl who witnesses her grandfather being treated unfairly, threatened, and even assaulted for trying to register to vote and her own narrative of being able to register and vote when old enough because of his efforts. For many Black girls in real life and in fiction, daring to dream is built on the foundation of other's struggles and comes from the ability to witness and offer testimony to those journeys as well. May the light of their legacies continue to shine on everyone who reads.

Recess: Stories in Black Girlhood Culture

> Now I feel like I have something to do with my life. I have something
> to work on. I have a goal.
>
> —Brooke Sheppard, *Sisters on Track*

In the eighth episode of Season Three ("Frunchroom") of Lena Waithe's Showtime series *The Chi* (2019), teenage character Keisha has been returned home
from a traumatic abduction. The episode shows her looking for articles about
what has happened to her and the kidnapper, who is killed in his escape. Amy
Sherald's now-famous portrait of Michelle Obama hangs in a powerful scene
after a verbal exchange with one of her friends, which leads into Keisha learning that she has lost her scholarship to college after everything else that she has
been through. Afterward, her younger brother Kevin and his friends Jake and
Poppa discuss being glad that God answers prayers over a vape pen.

There is a powerful family moment in which Keisha, Keven, their mother
(Mina), Jake, Poppa, and friends Everett and his mom Jada discuss whose
fault the kidnapping was over a meal that Keisha finally eats from the restaurant Everett is opening. Poppa ignites the exchange by trying to return cash
tips from her abductor, who frequented the restaurant where he works. The
question remains as to whether Keisha will be able to heal as she processes
with Jada, a social worker who has also experienced trauma, whether and
when her own healing will take place. "How long does it take before you feel
normal again?" Keisha asks. "Baby, if you waiting to feel normal again, you
gon' be waiting a long time," Jada responds. The series and the scene resonate
with Langston Hughes's noted poem "Harlem (A Dream Deferred)" with the
question, "What happens to a dream deferred?"

This poem became the substance of Lorraine Hansberry's *Raisin in the
Sun*, in which another young woman, Beneatha Younger, becomes the untold
story of deferred success. Although critical analysis of the play usually focuses
on her older brother, Walter Lee, whose inheritance through his mother (from
his late father's dream of supporting his family) is stolen in a deal gone wrong,
the unrealized dream in the story is that Beneatha wants to become a doctor.
What happens to Beneatha's dream?

In Amy Sherald's painting *All Things Bright and Beautiful* (2016), a young
girl stands against a bright yellow background, wearing a purple dress adorned
with teal and green flowers and hearts. She is looking into the light with her

hand held above her eyes to shield her from the brightness. How do we see Black girls in the light?

The light of the girls in this text cannot be dimmed—from fictional characters Maud Martha to the person Rosa, and then Nikki-Rosa, became. Born thirty-four years after Hansberry and a year after her death in the same city of Chicago, Illinois, Michelle LaVaughn Robinson Obama realized the dream of her parents, who raised her in a South Side Chicago home, made difficult choices so that she would earn a good education, and sent her to Princeton University. Obama later earned her advanced degree from Harvard University and had a fruitful legal career before meeting, mentoring, and then dating eventual Senator and President Barack Obama and making an eight-year life for their family in the White House and among the political establishment.

Beneatha's, and even Hansberry's, dream deferred was realized in a great way through Michelle Obama's story and the potential of her two daughters, Malia and Sasha, and of girls worldwide, as she tells in *Becoming*, but is not realized in all girlhood stories. The fictional Keisha laments not being able to leave Chicago now and is now "stuck" because of her circumstances, to which her rescuer responds by assuring her that she will get through it. "It's been a long road, but you've been the light at the end of it," he says, while warning her not to drown her sorrows in "brown liquor" and thanking her for giving his life meaning. She then packs her trophies and clothes in a trash bag, pours them into a bathtub with alcohol, and lights a fire as she watches her memories burn. "Maybe I wouldn't have gotten kidnapped if I wasn't wearing this shit," she tells her mother, who reassures her that nothing was her fault and mourned her inability to save her. "It's okay Ma," Keisha responds.

But what does getting through it look like for fictional and real girl protagonists? For Claireece "Precious" Jones, it is finding her path to literacy after her father rapes and impregnates her and finding no support either as a child or as a parent from her abusive mother. Precious, also the name of the film based on the book, also finds community in classmates at her new school who don't "fit in."

These stories become narratives of what E. Patrick Johnson might refer to as "quare" stories of Black girlhood and also represent the role of girls in the building of community. An even more contemporary example is 2021 film *Sisters on Track*, where three sisters who were runners survive housing displacement to set the foundation for their future through track. After the oldest girls get into a private school in New York with full scholarships, Coach Jean refers to a quote by Graham Greene, "This is that quote, 'when that door opens and lets your future in.'" The documentary transitions into Coach Jean leading the girls through a reading of *The Hate U Give*, asking if they would act and talk the same way at a White school. The girls talk about the perception of Black men as dangerous. "You gotta live [THUG LIFE] to survive where you live. . . otherwise you run track." When they worry that the school they got into may be closing, Coach Jean tells Tai, "You take on too much . . . for a little girl. Stop worrying." In the village model, she states, "if I have to take on a second job to pay tuition, I'll do it." She goes on to say, "running is what saves them," later stating that it was ingrained in her to take care of children who need extra help.

Meanwhile, Tai thinks through the pressure of running in order to go to college. Tai credits her for teaching that "even the little obstacles can affect your future." "I want this experience to mean something so I can prove that I'm capable . . . ." Along with her mother's influence, Coach Jean instills in her and other girls that they can do whatever they put their minds to.

These narratives are ones of survival, as girl protagonists in books, in film, and in real life survive through articulating who they are and where they belong. Through sports, through family influence, and through passion to build better worlds, they overcome obstacles placed in their way.

Toward a New Terrain

Shapeshifters must always stay on the side of change, possibility, movement, and the future, or they would not be so adept at shifting the normative shapes and spaces that threaten their (and our) lives. Shapeshifters must be optimists, or they wouldn't be able to make themselves and others whole in the face of narratives and practices meant to fragment, disembody, scatter, and confuse them.

—Aimee Meredith Cox, *Shapeshifters*

The only thing constant in the world is change.

—India.Arie, "Growth," from *Voyage to India*, ©2002 Motown Records

This book is both for and about the "shapeshifters," as Aimee M. Cox writes, "Black girls are . . . forced to confront their supposed inferiority and deviance on multiple intersecting and continually shifting social planes—adolescence being one of the critical places of intersection" (12). This tradition of confronting through movement began as early as with oral and documented narratives, from Phillis Wheatley's assertion of her "Ethiop" identity in her 1773 *Poems on*

Various Subjects, Religious and Moral through the graphic novel adaptation of Octavia Butler's profoundly foretelling representation of the apocalyptic years 2024 and 2025 in *Parable of the Sower*.

Contributing to a conversation that is also rooted in cultural contexts of shapeshifting across Indigenous, Japanese, and other cultures, Cox uses the term as a concept to discuss how African American girls resist the boundaries established for them by society. She argues:

> There are overlapping and mutually reinforcing similarities between the ideologies surrounding young people and the practices enacted to control them and the ideologies used to monitor and contain the lives of Blacks (especially Black women) through codes of respectability and boundaries of exclusion. These intersections complicate the ways in which young Black women mediate experiences in the public and private spheres. (12)

Intersectionality, the term coined by legal scholar and founder of the African American Policy Forum, Kimberle Crenshaw, has gained wide usage as the representation of multiple identities (race, gender, class, and age) and the ways in which they shape understanding, and it is an additional part of Black girl experiences, as Cox illustrates as well. Scholars across disciplines "have addressed the historical absenting of the experiences of girls in the context of youth cultural discourses, both in the academy and in popular culture" (12). Aria Halliday's collection of essays in *The Black Girlhood Studies Collection* discusses the multiple contexts of Black girls' presences and absences—in sociology, dance, music, and performance culture. Cox adds in *Shapeshifters* that the labor of Black girls is "not legitimized by the state" (14), and I add that it is often misread by any who refuse to see the ways in which Black girls not only contribute to but also shape society. She writes: "Black girls' presence changes the possibilities for what can occur in public and private spaces while also requiring us to see and understand these spaces differently" (25–26), adding that "The body, like the notion of home for these young women, can be by turns a space of safety and protection or one of instability and expulsion" (29).

Representations of Black girlhood in literature (including memoirs of no-longer-girls) require us to pay attention to Black girl bodies, throughout centuries and across media. Their narratives draw us to move, to relocate ourselves. Cox writes: "If we learn to pay a different type of attention to the ways young Black women move through and write their own worlds, failures and unfortunate outcomes may still offer blueprints for mapping a different world" (30), adding that their performances, both in everyday life and in formal performing arts, are "mutually definitive, embodied responses to the fundamental need to be seen and heard on one's own terms" (37). These stories all operate on their own terms but come together in a beautiful suite or performance as well.

What We Know

[W]e are so hungry for the morning/we're trying to feed our children the sun.
  —Ntozake Shange, "Bocas: A Daughter's Geography," 1983

I want to be great, I want to be known. So when I die, I want people to know who Rainn Sheppard was.
  —Rainn Sheppard, *Sisters on Track*

You're not the only one raising these girls.
  —Coach Jean, *Sisters on Track*

"Right On, Baby!"
  —Pearl Cleage, *Things I Should Have Told My Daughter*

In her collection of journal entries to her daughter, Deignan, who would be born later that year, playwright and novelist Pearl Cleage wrote on March 13, 1974:

I have let so many days go by. Tsk, tsk. What an awful mother already! . . . It is also weird for people to respond the way they do. Gloria Gayles says to me: "Are you excited?" I went into my standard response about how I was pleased and looking forward to it, etc. "yes," she said with obvious concern, "but are you excited?" I didn't really know what to say. I am not really "excited." Excited suggests an all-consuming elation that I do not have time to have! (44)

In her journal, Cleage states that altering one's style and life to become a "big glowing maternal being" is "negative to you and the kid": "How can he or she possibly survive the strain of having to be EVERYTHING in the mother's life? I am not getting down what I mean, but it is hard to figure it out. I mean, it is good to be having a baby, but it is not the be all/end all of my life. There!" (44). Although she resists needing the child to be everything and vice versa, she also begins to express concern for the care of the child: "I am already thinking that the two-month leave won't work. I want to see the kid grow for a while. I ought to be there to help it grow and get humanoid before we throw it into a nursemaid's arms. But there is time to figure it all out" (45).

Her chronicles of appreciating the baby's movement and hormones and humor speak to the complicated notions of pregnancy as part of identity, as she adds:

> April 10, 1974
>
> Just a brief note to say that last night about 9:30 after a hearty meal of two egg rolls and some shrimp fried rice, the lil' baby moved for the first time!!! I felt it and Michael could feel it, too. It was really hip. Felt like a little stretch was going on in there. . . . It really was such a positive feeling. I feel very good right through here about the whole thing. I think things will work out and we will all kind of mesh together and it won't be intrusive at all. Hooray! So let me note this for the baby book: April 9, 1974; felt first real movement. Right on, baby!" (46)

It is both the center and not, both the way she chooses to live and doesn't. As an expectant mother, Cleage is aware of how she feels including her own presentation. She writes, "I want to smoke a joint, but I am afraid of rearranging my child's lil' genes or something, so I won't do it" (46) and follows with, "I am . . . making a concerted effort to overrule my hormones and be Miss Sweetness and Light. Thinking sweet thoughts to have a sweet baby!" (47). She projects what she wants the child to experience even differently from her own life:

> I wish peace and health to this lil' kid. I want it to live forever and be perfect. Isn't that a burden to put on a baby who is as yet only six pre-natal months old? Ha! Already a pushy mother! (48).

She also notes emotions "between a kind of soft euphoria and a deep sense of dread at the thought of having responsibility for this lil' baby" (48). She describes the information from her own mother that "labor is a snap," which calms her nerves and comes up with a plan to accept collect calls for Frederick Douglass only if the baby is there (53) and days later, "August 7, 1974. . . . Fingers are crossed. That is the trip of the last few weeks. You are just READY to have the baby. Come on. Frederick Douglass!" (54)

Connecting the past even as a joke to her present, Cleage narrates the birthing of a daughter, Deignan Njeri Kristin Cleage Lomax, on August 30, 1974. Cleage writes: "I'm so glad she's a girl! . . . Welcome to the world, little baby! We've been waiting for you!!" (57). Deignan becomes part of the "continuing cycle from the slaves and the masters to our recently compiled family tree to the Africans before that on through Nanny and Poppy, Grandmother and grandfather. It's like you have added your own bit to our family to keep it going and be sure it survives" (58). As she continues her work for Mayor Maynard Jackson Jr., even nursing as she works on the mayor's remarks, Cleage also reflects on the legacy that she is passing on. "Deignan was nursing so she didn't seem to mind. She probably thinks all mothers do this" (59). Days later, she notes, "Deignan is one week old and thriving! I feel good, too" (59).

Writing in the journal allows her to note the good, bad, and in between of her life, as she states, "I do feel a little overwhelmed. A little insecure. I feel like I have to be super mom, super wife, always smiling, cute, etc. I know I shouldn't feel that way, but I do. I'm sure I'll get it together. Good grief! She's only just one week old!" (59). Cleage notes the dual pressure on her (and, possibly, also that will be passed to her daughter) to do everything. She cites her postpartum depression, which she calls a "blue funk" and how she feels better when she is able to reengage with her circle.

> We went to a party at John and Lillian Lewis's house with David and Shirley Franklin. I feel a lot better. We are thinking now of me going back to work at the end of October. I don't think Deignan will freak out. I will only be working a few hours a day at first so I can still breastfeed. I know this for sure: I have to have my own head straight and my own feelings sorted out or I'll be a rotten mother, wife, person, etc . . . I feel like my life is sorting itself out again and not racing too fast for me to catch it. (60)

Her friend Joanne is also struggling at home with a new baby, and Cleage writes, "I can't be a full time wife and mother. I think one of the reasons I'm coming out of the blue funk is that I realize it is almost October and I'll be back at work soon" (61). Between the dependence of the baby and adjusting to life as a spouse with a child to feeling guilty when Deignan gets sick, Cleage also notes moments of joy when she engages with the world outside of her home, seeing Stevie Wonder, and purchasing Leontyne Price albums.

We do not get Deignan's narrative in the book, which is Cleage's journaling as she tries to make sense of the interstices between human and woman and working mother and spouse, but I imagine that these moments of joy, both felt and documented, even amid the adjustment for Cleage, had an impact. Cleage, a mover in her own right as she published several books that include award-winning novels and plays, including *Blues for an Alabama Sky*

(1995) and *Flyin West* (1994), is able to show the vulnerability of just existing in *Things I Should Have Told My Daughter*, and fortunately, she still got the chance to.

The plight, and also the potential, of Black women (writers and otherwise) has been the ability and opportunity to sort out our own lives as we pass the baton. We are also, at the same time, passing the light to our daughters while keeping our own fires (and lights) burning. As a Black woman of a middle generation, between the Black Power era of my parents and the TikTok generation of my children (and having grown up with my grandmothers and even great-grandmothers born in the 1910s through 1930s), my charge is to sustain, enhance, and never dull the flames of activism (both organized and organic). As a scholar and a writer, my job is not only to tell stories but also to make sure that they remain vital parts of our culture

On Being Born: "The Birthday Party"

I don't remember my first birthday party—I heard that there was one when I was two, but I got chicken pox—but I do remember celebrating and being celebrated as a child. There was somebody's party when we lived in the Texas desert; I remember climbing into one of those station wagons with the back that opened out and going to some pizza place (probably Godfather's) with friends that we made in our military town. There was a McDonald's birthday party at some young age before my younger siblings were born—I assume that with it came a party package, because I remember a longest French fry contest and stacking then-styrofoam containers on top of each other to see who could build the tallest tower. There is one picture of me at a table outside our home with friends—I assume that it was in kindergarten, and my birthday is around Easter, so we were dressed colorfully with white socks (the ones that folded over with the lace)—decorating the tea cake shortbread cookies that my paternal grandmother, Vanilla (real name), always made.

I always joked that my mother had so many kids that she couldn't remember birthdays. That was not entirely true with just four of us, but it was certainly overwhelming to plan throughout the year. Instead of annual birthday parties, sometimes on our birthdays or half-birthdays at six months, we would stop at Baskin-Robbins and pick up an ice cream cake. Mint chocolate chip was a family favorite. With four children, you never needed others around to make it a celebration, and that was ours. I do remember the younger siblings getting Showbiz Pizza (now Chuck E. Cheese) parties with pizza and cake and that it didn't really matter whose birthday it was within our tight community of families and friends.

The next party I remember was in sixth grade, once I convinced my mother to let me have a "real" party (outside of the house/family). We agreed on the skating rink, and I could pass out ten invitations. I went to a school that was fifth through twelfth grades combined, so I didn't have the awkward start to middle school, but there was a new boy whom I will call L. Always what people called a tomboy (and now identifying within the beautiful spectrum of quareness), I invited girl and guy friends equally. On the last invitation, I hesitated—would he come? Not because I had any romantic feelings but more because I wanted to be included. "A skate party—cool," was the response I got. And I literally don't remember if he came or not. I don't think so, but I remember the sleepover of my girlfriends afterward—the laughs, giggles, the fun.

I hold these moments because they say that I was here, I was a child, and life, in those moments, was good.

Born
Those born caulless are
still gifted with vision to
see beyond this world.— j. b. lewis

Epilogue
Reading Play as Resistance

As an educator in university and K–12 classrooms and in community spaces, I have been called on lately to dialogue directly with youths on various forms of Black childhood, girlhood, and freedom that connect me back to these early experiences of my own childhood dreams. The connections have been through stories, although I continue to wonder what I have to say to this generation that is both different from and similar to my own. I am also a parent of a now nine-year-old, dynamic, girl-identified child and a twelve -year-old, tremendous, boy-identified child who defy the ways that society fix their identities. How do I tell them and teach them to be, as Charlene Carruthers describes it, "unapologetic" in this world? Additionally, during a time of global pandemic with COVID-19 that has disrupted but also rerouted learning for Black children, how do we help them make academic progress but also learn about themselves and preserve who they are?

My syllabus for my liberal studies course for first-year students, "Growing Up in America," did this for a number of years, through the centering of unapologetic stories of people and especially girls of color. Students of a variety of different racial, ethnic, class, and age backgrounds read *The Bluest Eye*, Sapphire's *Push*, and Angie Thomas's *The Hate U Give* to talk about what social justice is and whether it is even possible for these fictional Black girls.

Within the spectrum of representation, girl-identified characters in these texts see the dynamics of violence around them in significant ways, including the experience of sexual abuse and witnessing of physical abuse resulting. They use dreams or imagine other ways of being to move beyond the real or everyday trauma they cannot escape.

I also, however, think back to my experiences of Zora Neale Hurston's *Their Eyes Were Watching God* and Richard Wright's *Native Son*, both required in my eleventh-grade year. My classes usually begin with nineteenth-century African American women writers and move in some way to the present. Even what I represent as adolescent literature is usually about African American authors (including Frederick Douglass and Harriet Jacobs in their quests for freedom) at adolescent stages. Students relate to these authors for their messages of what "success" looks like (learning to read, seeking freedom), but they don't necessarily relate the themes of Black girlhood to their own experiences.

And why should they? Do the texts we choose, texts that are increasingly canonized and popularized, speak to their lives (and if so, how)? The framework of looking beyond typical experiences to responses that stretch both the characters and the society in which they live, enables this connection. For example, Black girlhood remembrance can facilitate a Black radical feminist critique in which Angie Thomas's protagonist Starr Carter cannot remain silent in the face of racialized violence. Critical reading steeped in Black girlhood remembrance of *The Hate U Give*, for example, can also allow white American students to see whiteness in ways that don't necessarily idealize their experiences. The students at Garden Heights (Starr's white private high school) don't understand Starr's narrative, and even her white boyfriend Chris doesn't always "get" her, although the distance is closed somewhat by the end of the book when Chris helps Starr and her family get out of the store that is being burned by King, who has a class-based vendetta against Starr's father, Maverick.

Students who come from Black communities also might not necessarily relate to Starr's option to go to a white private school. Likewise, some students find *Push* important but difficult to read, especially with the physical and emotional violence with which they may or may not be familiar. Through these texts, I think about what students need to know and how we get that to them. How do we support those who experience what we may see in these texts? Do they have the context to talk about anticapitalism or theoretical frameworks when, as with Janie Crawford and marriage, the world is telling them that the more they have, the better they are (or better able to achieve)?

Ultimately, how do we reaffirm the humanity of Black girls in our current social and political world with stories that are relevant to them? In *We Want to Do More than Survive* (2019), Bettina Love names the "spirit murder" that takes place in classrooms and communities. "More than survival" looks like Black girls challenging educators to decolonize curricula that was not made for them and their own abilities to connect histories in which Black children created and found support, even in segregated educational spaces, and change them into contemporary spaces where they can feel free. It looks like dreaming along with and beyond the circumstances of our children and, specifically, those of our girls, whose notions of freedom on an ordinary day look like something extraordinary and even excessive to most people. It looks like believing in #BlackGirlMagic while embracing the reality of Black girls' quotidian lives. It looks like, from Ntozake Shange's original and innovative choreopoem of the mid-1970s, which is still relevant today, singing for and with "colored girls who have considered suicide when the rainbow is enuf."

In her 2018 book, *How Long 'til Black Future Month?* (its name taken from her "shameless paean" to Janelle Monae), N. K. Jemisin talks about how hard it has been to love science fiction and fantasy as a black woman. "How terrifying it's been to realize *no one thinks my people have a future*. And how gratifying to finally accept myself and begin spinning the futures I want to see." She concludes with the directive: "There's the future over there. Let's all go" (xii). This book focused on how Black girls, as Black women, narrated their activism and imagine(d) themselves in other worlds through creative literature. Reflecting on the story of Lauren Olamina in Octavia Butler's *Parable of the Talents* (and the connection to her daughter in *Parable of the Sower*), I think about how Black girlhood is imagined in futuristic spaces. I argue that imagining spaces of liberation requires our ability to move beyond the present to think about the possibilities of life, of movement, of freedom. From Black girls' dreams to Afrofuturistic visions of Black girlhood, *Light and Legacies* asks: What might we imagine about narratives of Black childhood, and specifically Black girlhood, as freedom? What might it take to allow that freedom to exist?

> *Make Believe*
> Let's pretend we never met
> Just two ships passing in the ocean
> Sea-lengths away.
>
> I saw your sail though
> White, waving
> Flag of liberation.
>
> You didn't leave me behind.—j. b. lewis

"We Dream in Stories"

These are the stories by which we live, the stories told and written by our elders and foremothers. They are also the stories by which and with which they have lived.

On Black Girlhood
For those whose experiences will never lie
At the center
Of America's
Consciousness;
For whom vision is
Life,
Abundant.
We speak from margins
And call them
Home.
(j. b. lewis, 2021)

This is not a lost poem
For she was never irretrievable
But a found poem
For she discovered
Her story.

P.S.S. The Right to Play: Protecting Black Joy

Mommy, Can you play with me?

—Delany Lewis, daughter, 2020–21

Our ancestors hold us from within our own bodies. Guiding us through our reflections. . . . Light, refracted

—Beyoncé, *Black Is King*

Girl put your records on, tell me your favorite song
You go ahead, let your hair down
Sapphire and faded jeans
I hope you get your dreams
Just go ahead, let your hair down.

—Corinne Bailey Rae, "Put Your Records On," 2006

My oldest child, the Virgo, the one who worries and is cautious about everything, turned ten on August 23, 2020, still in the midst of the COVID-19 pandemic. The way our birthdays are set up in my family (from April to August), every single member of our household celebrated at least one and sometimes two "COVID birthdays" so far. At first, making plans was fun. I was April 2020—had a Zoom cocktail hour and girlfriend chat, made a private beach in my backyard, got a bicycle, and practiced yoga steadily for a couple months (and, sadly, haven't picked it back up since spring). Early July was the birth month of my then-seven-year-old, who wanted to fish on family property (and sat under the tent playing games on her phone), camp like Barbie (shout-outs to friends who lent a camper for the afternoon), and scoot through the neighborhood. My spouse got a mountain trip, and the most recent, cautious child got a beach trip (which turned into a pool trip so he can actually see through the water), a socially distanced hike, and all his favorite meals. I have also "treated myself" with beautiful drives; virtual and occasionally distanced time with friends; and most recently, a masked massage and manicure for making it through five months and four birthdays. We have, as a family, tried to play despite ongoing difficult circumstances.

It was my strongest desire that my family (and, honestly, that I) remember something positive from this spring and summer, this strange, sad, and unending season where we, like many others, lost a family member before his time; saw the public death of a Black man on television; heard about the deaths of many others taken publicly and in their homes (with the murderers of Breonna Taylor and now those who attacked Jacob Blake roaming free); had plans, events, and school programs canceled; and went months without leaving the house, only to be told that it may never be truly safe to re-emerge for at least a year. Play, usually near home but occasionally away or with family, and always what we hope is a safe enough distance from other people, has been our only space of freedom.

As an academic scholar, community educator, and parent, I have thought and written about freedom for now over a decade. First, it was the freedom of Black women to write the terms of their liberation even when society did not. Black women writers such as Phillis Wheatley; Harriet Jacobs (who hid in a garret in her grandmother's house for seven years, watching her children through cracks in the exterior until she could escape to freedom); enslaved-persons-turned-educators Ellen Craft and Anna Julia Cooper; my hometown (Augusta, Georgia) heroine Lucy Craft Laney, who spoke freedom to learn into the lives of her pupils at Haines Institute which she founded; and others orchestrated their own narratives of movement through spaces that were never meant for them. Freeborn Charlotte Forten (Grimke) wrote to connect freedom she didn't feel to Black communities who were just realizing their freedom day by day as "contraband" in the Sea Islands in the early 1860s. Writer-speaker-activist Frances Ellen Watkins Harper imagined freedom for the subjects of her poetry and novels in the nineteenth century.

Now, I write about the freedom of Black children to play, a project that was honestly stunted, if not fully paused, by the multiple pandemics of 2020. Where, I ask, do Black children find the space and the right to move freely when Tamir Rice, Trayvon Martin, Bresha Meadows (whose murder of her father after reportedly surviving domestic violence has been contested in and out of court), and countless others had their childhoods arrested or ended by circumstances that did not see them as children or even as human beings? My work has turned to fiction as ways to imagine different possibilities, but from the late Toni Morrison's 1970 bestseller *The Bluest Eye* to Sapphire's *Push* (1996), to Angie Thomas's *The Hate U Give* (2017), we know that even fictional characters endure the worst circumstances to have their stories told.

So now, we the parents, we the educators, we the community members, are left with the charges of safety, of healing, and of wellness for Black children. It is a task that is, at times, daunting, as many of our parents and community members have been called out of homes to various careers and jobs of service to others. We are first responders, caregivers, teachers, managers, facilities workers, food service employees, and the list goes on. We also, sadly, question the safety of our children when left only to depend on the goodwill of others. This question of safety is not a new pandemic, as we worried about educational environments that did not support our children and public exposure that did not protect them even before the current health and racial tumult. We navigated the hierarchy of schools in our community, choosing an allegedly "good" system but frustrated by the lack of diversity in our assigned schools (and making a decision that we have always appreciated in a magnet program that allowed for both).

From college student athlete to newly minted doctorate in educational leadership, my spouse has also been a role model for our children as the primary home educator while working and in school for most of their lives, whereas my position as faculty previously allowed travel for research and public presentations. They also know that I am an educator and administrator, they see my work at home and at conferences (which they have even joined as schedules allow), and they have spent hours on both of our campuses, seeing that there were numerous possibilities for children who look like them. This is unfortunately not the norm for all Black children. Although some children of all races can go an entire academic career without seeing a Black teacher at the front of the classroom, and even make it to college, if that far, without seeing a Black man, woman, or nonbinary head of classroom, it is important for us to show both that learning starts at home and that Black parents are present in public school and academic settings as well. We may not have the collective economic resources of paid pods of learning, but we have always had our villages of support in informal and even in formal educational spaces.

The question is, as health and racial pandemics continue, will the world ever truly protect Black children at play? Will masks in the name of safety continue to allow for the sanctioned discrimination against them? Will they be bound by restrictions of seeing peers of different races flourish while being told that they cannot, falling further behind in the name of progress? Will they be seen and recognized, on virtual learning platforms, and in public spheres, even as their parents are murdered in front of their faces? Will they be forced to believe that they can only become heroes beyond this earth?

In a panel called "Making Our Way" in March 2022 that discussed how programs in the field of women's, gender, and sexuality studies in two North Carolina universities navigate chaos of the academy and society in general, three Black-woman-identified scholars noted the pressure for women to make better lives for everyone while being impacted themselves by the turbulence of multiple pandemics. Scholar and instructor J. Tiffany Holland noted the reminders of "trying to deal day to day with constant reminders of immortality" and the need to "radically [try] to get our lives," leaning into "community and interdependence." We have to "lean into the idea of change and creativity," asking ourselves, "What are the ways there has been mass creativity in . . . hellscape?" As we do so, Holland expanded, we have to ask what is giving us joy? Dr. Charmaine Lang, educator and chief of staff for the National Association of Working Women organization 9to5, continued with suggestions to use personal support networks, pausing, and pleasure as care, along with spirituality, therapy, rest, and nourishing food.

I hosted a viewing event for my college students in a class that Wednesday night, many of them women and just a few of them Black women. Through conversations such as this on self-care in community, how Black women writers of the South created and sought spaces for healing, and taking breaks (with scholar Sharon Hayes-Brown articulating, "I want to curate a life where I don't need a break," and Dr. Lang ending with the statement, "We still in here"). And indeed, we are. We survive in our communities, by curating and preserving black girlhood archives, and by, as Holland stated, "be[ing] creative in doing something new . . . [as] we know what we've been doing doesn't work at any percent."

We get to brilliant Black girl futures through dreams, through spaces to move and perform, through creating literary and even fugitive life spaces for Black girls to believe that they are, have, and can be whatever they need. We move from Octavia Butler's acknowledgment of Black woman and girl futurity in *Parable of the Sower* and *Parable of the Talents* to Jacqueline Woodson thinking about dreamscapes both in urban spaces of her mother and in the Greenville, South Carolina, "country" of her grandparents, and to in Maddy wanting to have and do "everything, everything" in the book of that name by Nicola Yoon. I argue through these texts that imagining spaces of liberation of and for Black girls requires our ability to move beyond the present to think about the possibilities of life, of movement, of freedom.

For that freedom to exist, we return to the requiems of earlier texts to think about those same bodies moving through spaces. From enslavement, what about those who, to borrow June Jordan's book title, "did not die," at least in spirit? The four little girls whose bodies were attacked in Birmingham, Alabama, on September 16, 1963; those who disappeared in the Atlanta child murders of 1979–81; and the trans women whose names grow on lists while their stories remain mysteries?

To recover these stories, we have to remember, to dramatize, to document. We then move beyond fixed spaces to find the freedom of girlhood dreams, traced through narratives of space travel, through *Mae Among the Stars*, *Hidden Figures*, and others where the stories of astronaut Mae Jemison, mathematician Katherine Johnson, and others are told. We also reimagine travel through time and space with the narratives of Phillis Wheatley, published in 1773 under the authority of her master and several White men (ministers, politicians, etc.) who barely made it possible for her to tell her own story in her way as the story of an Ethiop, as she refers to herself in her literary journey to find and share her sense of self. We find narratives of escape, character, and triumph, of biographical lives often gifted with extraordinary characteristics to survive, narratives of the future, or space, and beyond.

After the Civil Rights Acts of 1964 and 1965, where federal funding was poured into the publication of texts that were not necessarily positive and sometimes downright racist and stereotypical representations of Black childhood, we get to the future through narratives of return, such as the flying diasporic figures of Virginia Hamilton's *The People Could Fly*. We find ourselves in the neoslave narratives of the 1980s that imagine different endings besides death although, per Hamilton and others, death is also a type of freedom. We are even on *Sesame Street* of 1969–2019 and beyond, imagining that kids in urban spaces could move through their imaginations, and *Reading Rainbow*, encouraging us to "take a look, it's in a book" in the 1980s and 1990s. It is using the eyes of a child to see a better world.

As Woodson represents in *Brown Girl Dreaming*, dreams are also ways in which Black girls move away from visions of Black girlhood that have been created for them toward transformative justice, through dreams of freedom and imagining different pathways. They are narratives found in stories told to children that resist the boundaries of a "simple" childhood. They are stories that move us from southern to northern to outer spaces, stories that transcend histories and move across generations.

Black children, and inherently Black girls, dream of different ways of being, of existing, and these dreams are represented in a literary canon of Black women writers. There are Isie Watts and Janie Crawford of Zora Neale Hurston's imagination, who want to travel the world and escape the bounds of girlhood and domesticity. There is Toni Morrison's Nel Wright, who sees a future beyond her mother's control, and Pecola Breedlove, whose eyes finally become blue enough (if only in her own mind) to escape what she has seen.

We are left with more questions than answers: What does radical creativity look like as we move into a Black-girl-centered future? When will Black children be fully able to celebrate the lives they have without fear? And in the meantime, where can they also find freedom to play? Finally (but not the end), where are the spaces where Black girlhood is realized, and what remains unseen in the ways in which we engage their stories?

Appendix

A Blackgirl Booklist

For the past three to four years, I have traveled with these books. They have been in my work bag, my purse, my car, beside (and even read in) my bed. I have lived with the Black girl characters. I have created and constructed bibliographies of their narratives in my mind, a Blackgirl reading list to which I return often. This list in not conclusive, but it does scratch the surface of what and who Black girl protagonists can be and what their authors reveal to the world. Thank you to these authors for sharing their work. May all of these narratives, real and imagined, continue to be lights along the journey.

They are as follows:

Angelou, Maya. *I Know Why the Caged Bird Sings*. New York: Random House, 1969.

Bambara, Toni Cade, ed. *The Black Woman: An Anthology*. New York: Signet Press, 1970.

———. *Gorilla, My Love*. New York: Vintage Books, 1992.

———. *The Salt Eaters*. New York: Vintage Books, 1992.

———. *These Bones Are Not My Child*. New York: Pantheon Books, 1999.

Butler, Octavia E. *Parable of the Sower*. New York: Grand Central, 1993.

———. *Parable of the Talents*. New York: Grand Central, 1998.

———. *Wild Seed*. New York: Grand Central, 1980.

Giovanni, Nikki. "Nikki-Rosa." *The Selected Poems of Nikki Giovanni: 1968–1995*. New York: William Morrow, 1996.

———. *Rosa*. New York: Square Fish, 2005.

Hurston, Zora Neale. *Their Eyes Were Watching God*. New York: HarperCollins, 1937.

Jones, Tayari P. *Leaving Atlanta*. New York: Warner Books, 2002.

———. *Silver Sparrow: A Novel*. Chapel Hill, NC: Algonquin Books of Chapel Hill, 2012.

Meriwether, Louise. *Daddy Was a Number Runner*. New York: Feminist Press, 1970.

Morrison, Toni. *The Bluest Eye*. New York: Vintage Books, 1970.

———. *Sula*. New York: Vintage Books, 1973.

Sapphire. *Push*. New York: Vintage Books, 1996.

Shakur, Assata. *Assata: An Autobiography*. Chicago: Lawrence Hill Books, 1987.

Shange, Ntozake. *Betsey Brown: A Novel*. New York: St. Martin's Press, 1995.

———. *for colored girls who have considered suicide/when the rainbow is enuf*. New York: Scribner, 1975.

Thomas, Angie. *The Hate U Give*. New York: Balzer + Bray, 2017.

———. *On the Come Up*. New York: Balzer + Bray, 2019.

And on and on. . . .

Bibliography

Special reading note: In memory of memories, specifically, Toni Morrison's *The Bluest Eye, Sula, Jazz, and Tar Baby*, found on my mother's shelves at home (along with Terry McMillan's *Disappearing Acts* and *Waiting to Exhale*, which I brought to Friday reading in seventh grade and my teacher, Ms. Berger, never batted an eye). I remember reading both James Baldwin's *If Beale Street Could Talk* and Morrison's *Paradise* in the high school library, checking them out again and again until I finished both (and sometimes reading more than once). In the early 2000s, I led a girls' book club at a Black Baptist church in Evanston, Illinois, and I am grateful to those girls (and their parents) for reading many of them with me. These texts were gifts to my perception of Black girlhood.

Ahmed, Roda. *Mae Among the Stars*. New York: Harper, 2018.

Angelou, Maya. *I Know Why the Caged Bird Sings*. New York: Random House, 1969.

———. *Letter to My Daughter*. New York: Random House Trade Paperbacks, 2009.

Baldwin, James. *The Evidence of Things Not Seen*. New York: Henry Holt, 1995.

Bambara, Toni Cade, ed. *The Black Woman: An Anthology*. New York: Signet Press, 1970.

———. *Gorilla My Love*. New York: Vintage Books, 1992.

———. *Salt Eaters*. New York: Vintage Books, 1992.

———. *Those Bones Are Not My Child*. New York, Pantheon Books, 1999.

Bretherton, Inge, ed. "Introduction." In *Symbolic Play: The Development of Social Understanding*. Orlando, FL: Academic Press, 1984, 1.

———. "Representing the Social World in Symbolic Play: Reality and Fantasy." In *Symbolic Play: The Development of Social Understanding*. Orlando, FL: Academic Press, 1984, 3.

Bridges, Ruby. *Through My Eyes*. New York: Scholastic Press, 1999.

Brooks, Gwendolyn. *Family Pictures*. Detroit: Broadside, 1971.

———. *Maud Martha, a Novel*. New York: Harper, 1953.

———. "To the Young Who Want to Die." In *Children of Promise*. New York: Harry N. Abrams, 1991.

brown, adrienne maree. "Radical Love and Liberation." "Permission to Imagine: Radical Love & Pleasure" Lecture presented December 5, 2020. CTZNWell (virtual).

Brown, Charlotte Hawkins. *The Correct Thing to Do, To Say, To Wear*. Durham, NC: The Seeman Printery, 1941.

Brown, Elaine. *A Taste of Power*. New York: Penguin Books, 2021.

Brown, Ruth Nicole. *Black Girlhood Celebration: Toward a Hip-Hop Feminist Pedagogy*. New York: Peter Lang, 2009.

Boyce, Jo Ann Allen and Debbie Levy. *This Promise of Change: One Girl's Story in the Fight for School Equality*. New York: Bloomsbury Children's Books, 2019.

Carruthers, Charlene. *Unapologetic: A Black, Queer, and Feminist Mandate for Radical Movements*. Boston: Beacon Press, 2018.

Calmenson, Stephanie and Joanna Cole. *Miss Mary Mack and Other Street Rhymes*. New York: HarperCollins, 1990.

Childress, Alice. *Rainbow Jordan*. New York: Avon, 1982.

Clark-Robinson, Monica, and Frank Morrison. *Let the Children March*. Illustrated by Frank Morrison. Boston: Houghton Mifflin Harcourt, 2018.

Cleage, Pearl. "An Evening with Nikki Giovanni," HistoryMakers, June 2005.

———. *Things I Should Have Told My Daughter: Lies, Lessons & Love Affairs*. New York: Atria Books, 2014.

Cooper v. Aaron, 358 US 1 (1958).

Cox, Aimee Meredith. *Shapeshifters: Black Girls and the Choreography of Citizenship*. Durham, NC: Duke University Press, 2015.

Cullors, Patrisse. *When They Call You a Terrorist: A Black Lives Matter Memoir*. New York: St. Martin's Press, 2018.

Davis, Angela. *Are Prisons Obsolete*. New York: Seven Stories Press, 2003.

———. *Freedom Is a Constant Struggle: Ferguson, Palestine, and the Foundations of a Movement*. Chicago: Haymarket Books, 2015.

———. *If They Come in the Morning: Voices of Resistance*. The Third Press, 1971.

———. *Women, Race and Class*. New York: Random House, 1981.

Davis, Angela Y., and Joy James, ed. *The Angela Y. Davis Reader*. Malden, MA: Blackwell, 1998.

"Dr. Charlotte Hawkins Brown," North Carolina Historic Sites, https://historicsites .nc.gov, accessed August 26, 2022.

Equiano, Olaudah. *The Interesting Narrative of the Life of Olaudah Equiano, or Gustavus Vassa, the African, Written by Himself*. digireads.com, 1789, 2001.

Evans, Mari. *I Am a Black Woman*. New York: William Morrow, 1970.

Farinde, Abiola A., Tempestt Adams, and Chance W. Lewis, "Segregation Revisited: The Racial Education Landscape of Charlotte Mecklenburg Schools." *The Western Journal of Black Studies* 38, no. 3 (2014): 177–83.

Flournoy, Valerie. *The Patchwork Quilt*. New York: Scholastic Press (by arrangement with Dial Books for Young Readers), 1985.

Ford, Tanisha. *Dressed in Dreams: A Black Girl's Love Letter to the Power of Fashion*. New York: St. Martin's Press, 2019.

"Four Black Schoolgirls Killed in Birmingham Church Bombing," HISTORY, Originally published February 9, 2010; accessed August 25, 2022. https://www.history .com/this-day-in-history/four-black-schoolgirls-killed-in-birmingham.

Garbus, Liz, dir. *What Happened, Miss Simone?* Los Gatos, CA: Netflix, 2015. Aired June 26, 2015.

Gaunt, Kyra D. *The Games Black Girls Play: Learning the Ropes from Double-Dutch to Hip-Hop.* New York: New York University Press, 2006.

Giovanni, Nikki. *Black Feeling, Black Talk/Black Judgement.* New York: William Morrow, 1970.

———. "Ego Tripping." In *The Selected Poems of Nikki Giovanni: 1968–1995.* New York: William Morrow, 1996.

———. "Knoxville." In *The Selected Poems of Nikki Giovanni: 1968–1995.* New York: William Morrow, 1996.

———. "Nikki-Rosa." In *The Selected Poems of Nikki Giovanni: 1968–1995.* New York: William Morrow, 1996.

———. "Poem for a Lady of Leisure, Now Retired." William MorrowRecited, The HistoryMakers "An Evening with Nikki Giovanni" interview with Pearl Cleage. Recorded June 18, 2005, Atlanta, GA.

———. "Shine." William MorrowRecited, The HistoryMakers "An Evening with Nikki Giovanni" interview with Pearl Cleage. Recorded June 18, 2005, Atlanta, GA.

———. "Woman Poem." In *The Selected Poems of Nikki Giovanni: 1968–1995.* New York: William Morrow, 1996.

———. *Rosa.* New York: Square Fish, 2005.

———. *Spin a Soft Black Song.* New York: Farrar, Straus and Giroux, 1987.

Goeller, Bria, and Good Trubble. *That Little Girl Was Me.* 2020. Photograph.

Green, Molette. "'Fifth Little Girl' in Birmingham Church Bombing Tells Harrowing Tale," originally published February 8, 2021; accessed August 25, 2022. https:// www.nbcwashington.com/.

Green, Naima. "The Perfect Woman to Paint Michelle Obama," *New York Times,* November 5, 2017.

Griffin, Farah Jasmine. "Conflict and Chorus: Reconsidering Toni Cade's *The Black Woman: An Anthology.*" In *Is It Nation Time? Contemporary Essays on Black Power and Black Nationalism,* ed. Eddie S. Glaude Jr. (Chicago: University of Chicago Press, 2002), 113–29.

———. *Read Until You Understand: The Profound Wisdom of Black Life and Literature.* New York: W. W. Norton and Co., 2021.

Hackley, Emma Azalia. *The Colored Girl Beautiful.* Berkeley, CA: Mint Editions, 2021.

Halliday, Aria S. *The Black Girlhood Studies Collection.* Toronto, ON, Canada: Women's Press, 2019.

Hamilton, Virginia. *The People Could Fly: The Picture Book.* Illustrated by Leo Dillon and Diane Dillon. New York: Alfred A. Knopf, 2004.

Hansberry, Lorraine. *A Raisin in the Sun and Related Readings.* Evanston, IL: McDougal Littell, 1997.

Harper, Frances E. W. *Iola Leroy, Or Shadows Uplifted.* Boston: Beacon Press, 1987.

———. *Minnie's Sacrifice. Sowing and Reaping. Trial and Triumph: Three Rediscovered Novels* by Frances E. W. Harper. ed. Frances Smith Foster, 1869. Boston: Beacon Press, 1994.

Hartman, Saidiya V. *Lose Your Mother: A Journey Along the Atlantic Slave Route.* New York: Farrar, Straus and Giroux, 2007.

———. *Wayward Lives, Beautiful Experiments: Intimate Histories of Social Upheaval.* New York: W. W. Norton & Co., 2019.

"The History and Impact of Swann v. Charlotte-Mecklenburg." EducationNC, 2016, accessed June 8, 2021. https://www.ednc.org/the-history-and-impact-of-swann-v-charlotte-mecklenburg/.

Holland, Sharon Patricia, and Donald E. Pease. *Raising the Dead Readings of Death and (Black) Subjectivity.* Durham, NC: Duke University Press, 2000.

Holloway, Karla F. C. *Codes of Conduct: Race, Ethics, and the Color of Our Character.* New Brunswick, NJ: Rutgers University Press, 1995.

Hughes, Langston. "Genius Child." In *The Collected Works of Langston Hughes.* Columbia: University of Missouri Press, 2001.

———. "Harlem (Dream Deferred)." In *The Collected Works of Langston Hughes.* Columbia: University of Missouri Press, 2001.

———. "I, Too." In *The Collected Works of Langston Hughes.* Columbia: University of Missouri Press, 2001

———. "To Be Somebody." In *The Collected Works of Langston Hughes.* Columbia: University of Missouri Press, 2001.

Hurston, Zora Neale. Archive letters. Moorland-Spingarn Library, Howard University, Washington, DC.

———. "Drenched in Light." In *The Signet Classic Book of Short Stories,* edited by Dorothy Abbott and Susan H. Koppelman. New York: Signet Press, 1991.

———. "John Redding Goes to Sea." *The Stylus,* May 1921. Reprinted https://www.narrativemagazine.com/issues/stories-week-2016-2017/story-week/john-redding-goes-sea-zora-neale-hurston. Accessed August 26, 2022.

———. *Their Eyes Were Watching God.* New York: HarperCollins, 1937.

Jacobs, Harriet [as Linda Brent]. *Incidents in the Life of a Slave Girl: Written by Herself. 1861.* Orlando, FL: Harcourt Brace & Company, 1973.

———. *Incidents in the Life of a Slave Girl. 1861.* New York: W. W. Norton and Co., 2001.

Johnson, E. Patrick. "'Quare' Studies, or (Almost) Everything I Know about Queer Studies I Learned from My Grandmother." In *Black Queer Studies: A Critical Anthology,* edited by E. Patrick Johnson and Mae G. Henderson. Durham, NC: Duke University Press, 2005.

Jones, Tayari P. Leaving Atlanta. New York: WarnerBooks, 2002.

———. *Silver Sparrow: A Novel.* Chapel Hill, NC: Algonquin Books of Chapel Hill, 2012.

Jordan, June. *Some of Us Did Not Die: New and Selected Essays of June Jordan.* New York: Basic Civitas Books, 2002.

King, Martin Luther. "Eulogy for the Young Victims of the 16th Street Baptist Church Bombing" [Transcript]. September 18, 1963, Sixteenth Street Baptist Church, Birmingham, Alabama. https://mlkscholars.mit.edu/updates/2015/invoking-dr-king. Accessed August 26, 2022.

Lewin, Sarah. "'Hidden Figures' Explores NASA and Civil Rights History." SPACE.com, January 5, 2017. https://www.space.com/.

Lindsey, Treva B. *America Goddam: Violence, Black Women, and the Struggle for Justice.* Oakland: University of California Press, 2022.

Love, Bettina L. "Anti-Black State Violence, Classroom Edition: The Spirit Murdering of Black Children." *Journal of Curriculum and Pedagogy* 13, no. 1 (2016): 22–25.

———. *Hip Hop's Lil' Sistas Speak: Negotiating Hip Hop Identities and Politics in the New South.* New York: Peter Lang, 2005.

———. *We Want to Do More Than Survive: Abolitionist Teaching and the Pursuit of Educational Freedom.* Boston: Beacon Press, 2019.

Lorde, Audre. "And What About the Children?" In *The Collected Poems of Audre Lorde.* New York: W. W. Norton and Co., 1997.

———. *Cables to Rage.* London: Paul Breman, 1970.

———. "Naturally." In *The Collected Poems of Audre Lorde.* New York: W. W. Norton, 1997.

———. *Zami: A New Spelling of My Name.* Berkeley, CA: Crossing Press, 1982.

Meriwether, Louise. *Daddy Was a Number Runner.* New York: Feminist Press, 1970.

Mitchell, Margaree King. *Granddaddy's Gift.* New York: Scholastic Press, 1997.

Morris, Monique W. *Pushout: The Criminalization of Black Girls in Schools.* New York: The New Press, 2016.

———. *Sing a Rhythm, Dance a Blues: Education for the Liberation of Black and Brown Girls.* New York: The New Press, 2019.

Morrison, Toni. *The Bluest Eye.* New York: Vintage Books, 1970.

———. *Sula.* New York: Vintage Books, 1973.

Mullane, Deirdre, ed. *Crossing the Danger Water: Three Hundred Years of African-American Writing.* New York: Anchor Books, 1993.

Nazaryan, Alexander, "School Segregation in America Is as Bad Today as It Was in the 1960s," *Newsweek,* March 22, 2018. https://www.newsweek.com/2018/03/30/school-segregation-america-today-bad-1960-855256.html.

Neal, Mark Anthony. *Soul Babies: Black Popular Culture and the Post-Soul Aesthetic.* New York: Routledge, 2002.

Nemiroff, Robert, and Lorraine Hansberry. *To Be Young, Gifted, and Black: Lorraine Hansberry in Her Own Words.* New York: Signet Classics, 2011.

Obama, Michelle. *Becoming.* New York: Crown, 2018.

Parker, Morgan. *Who Put this Song On?* New York: Delacorte Press, 2019.

Parks v. LaFace Records, et al. 329 F.3d 437, Sixth Cir., 2003

Piaget, Jean. *Play, Dreams, and Imitation in Childhood.* New York: W. W. Norton, 1962.

Plunkett, Jake. *The Late Show with Stephen Colbert.* Season 6, episode 51, interview with Megan Thee Stallion. Aired December 9, 2020, on CBS. https://www.cbs.com/shows/the-late-show-with-stephen-colbert/.

Randolph-Wright, Charles, dir. *Mama, I Want to Sing!* 2012. Produced by Vision Films and CodeBlack Entertainment. Distributed by Fox Faith.

Ringgold, Faith. *Aunt Harriet's Underground Railroad in the Sky.* New York: Scholastic Press (with Crown Publishers), 1992.

Rockwell, Norman. *The Problem We All Live With* [painting], 1964. Oil on canvas, 91 cm × 150 cm. Norman Rockwell Museum, Stockbridge, MA.

Sanchez, Sonia, Dudley Randall, and Ademola Olugebefola. *We a baddDDD people.* Detroit: Broadside Press, 1970.

Sapphire. *Push.* New York: Vintage Books, 1996.

"Say Their Names Memorial," accessed August 25, 2022, https://www.saytheirnames memorials.com.

Shakur, Assata. *Assata: An Autobiography.* Chicago: Lawrence Hill Books, 1987.

Shange, Ntozake. *Betsey Brown: A Novel.* New York: St. Martin's Press, 1995.

———. *A Daughter's Geography.* New York: St. Martin's Press, 1984.

———. *for colored girls who have considered suicide/when the rainbow is enuf.* New York: Scribner, 1975.

Sherald, Amy. *All Things Bright and Beautiful,* 2016, oil on canvas, 54 × 43 in. (135.16 × 109.22 cm), collection of Frances and Burton Reifler, Winston-Salem, N.C. T.2018.23. Courtesy of the artist and Hauser & Wirth.

———. "Breonna Taylor: A Beautiful Life" (magazine cover), *Vanity Fair,* September 1, 2020.

Shetterly, Margot Lee. *Hidden Figures: The American Dream and the Untold Story of the Black Women Mathematicians Who Helped Win the Space Race.* New York: William Morrow, 2016.

———. *Hidden Figures: The True Story of Four Black Women and the Space Race.* New York: Harper, 2018.

———. *Hidden Figures Young Readers' Edition.* New York: HarperCollins, 2016.

Singer, Jerome L. *The Child's World of Make-Believe: Experimental Studies of Imaginative Play.* New York: Academic Press, 1973.

Spillers, Hortense J. "Mama's Baby, Papa's Maybe: An American Grammar Book." In *The Black Feminist Reader*, edited by Joy James and T. Denean Sharpley-Whiting, 57–87. Malden, MA: Blackwell Publishers, 2000.

Sullivan, Charles. *Children of Promise: African-American Literature and Art for Young People*. New York: Harry N. Abrams, 1991.

Sullivan, Mecca Jamillah. *Poetics of Difference: Queer Feminist Forms in the African Diaspora*. Chicago: University of Illinois Press, 2021.

Sutton-Smith, Brian. *The Ambiguity of Play*. Cambridge, MA: Harvard University Press, 2009.

Taylor, Keeanga-Yahmatta. *From #BlackLivesMatter to Black Liberation*. Chicago: Haymarket Books, 2016.

Taylor, Mildred D. *All the Days Past, All the Days to Come*. New York: Penguin Books, 2021.

———. *The Friendship* (First edition). New York: Puffin Books, 1987.

———. *Gold Cadillac*. New York: Puffin Books, 1998.

———. *The Land*. New York: Puffin Books, 2001.

———. *Let the Circle Be Unbroken*. New York: Puffin Books, 1981.

———. *The Road to Memphis*. New York: Puffin Books, 1990.

———. *Roll of Thunder, Hear My Cry*. New York: Puffin Books, 1976.

———. *Song of the Trees*. New York: Puffin Books, 2003.

———. *The Well: David's Story*. New York: Puffin Books, 1995.

Thomas, Angie. *The Hate U Give*. New York: Balzer + Bray, 2017.

———. *On The Come Up*. New York: Balzer + Bray, 2019.

Tillet, Salamishah. *In Search of the Color Purple: The Story of an American Masterpiece*. New York: Abrams Press, 2021.

Trethewey, Natasha. *Memorial Drive: A Daughter's Memoir*. New York, Ecco, 2020.

Truth, Sojourner. "Arn't I a Woman." In Henry Louis Gates and Valerie Smith. *The Norton Anthology of African American Literature*, third edition. New York: W. W. Norton, 2014.

van der Borch, Corinne, and Tone Grøttjord-Glenne, dirs. *Sisters on Track*. Los Gatos, CA: Netflix, 2021. Aired April 21, 2021.

Walker, Alice. *Absolute Trust in the Goodness of the Earth*. New York: Random House Trade, 2004.

———. *The Color Purple*. New York: Harcourt Brace Jovanovich, 1982.

———. *In Search of Our Mothers' Gardens: Womanist Prose* (1st ed.). New York: Harcourt Brace Jovanovich, 1983.

Walker, Margaret. *Prophets for a New Day*. Detroit: Broadside Press, 1970.

Wheatley, Phillis. *The Poems of Phillis Wheatley*. Chapel Hill: University of North Carolina Press, 1989.

————. *Poems on Various Subjects, Religious and Moral. 1773.*

Wilkinson, Jet. *The Chi.* Season 3, episode 8, "Frunchroom." Aired August 9, 2020, on Showtime. https://www.sho.com/the-chi/season/3/episode/8/frunchroom.

Woodson Jacqueline. *Brown Girl Dreaming.* New York: Penguin, 2014.

Wright, Nazera Sadiq. *Black Girlhood in the Nineteenth Century.* Chicago: University of Illinois Press, 2016.

Discography

Armstrong, Louis "What a Wonderful World." *What a Wonderful World.* Written by Bob Thiele (as "George Douglas") and George David Weiss, produced by Bob Thiele. United Recording, released as a single in 1967, reissued in 1988.

Carter, Beyoncé Knowles. "Brown Skin Girl." *The Lion King: The Gift* [Soundtrack]. Written by Beyoncé, Carlos St. John, Adio Marchant, Shawn Carter, P2J, Stacy Barthe, Anathi Mnyango, Michael Uzowuru, and Ayo Balogun; produced by Beyoncé, P2J, and Dixie. Parkwood-Columbia, released July 23, 2019.

India.Arie, "Growth." *Voyage to India.* Written by India Simpson, produced by India. Arie, Blue Miller, Paul Morton Jr., Andrew Ramsey, and Shannon Sanders. Motown Records, released September 24, 2002.

Rae, Corinne Bailey. "Put Your Records On." *Corinne Bailey Rae.* Written by Corinne Bailey Rae, John Beck, and Chrisanthou. EMI Records, released February 20, 2006.

Simone, Nina. "Backlash Blues." *Nina Simone Sings the Blues.* Written by Langston Hughes, produced by Danny Davis. RCA Records, released January 1, 1967.

————. "I Loves You Porgy." *Little Girl Blue.* Written by DuBose Hayward, George Gershwin, and Ira Gershwin. Bethlehem Records, released in February 1959.

————. "I Wish I Knew How It Would Feel to Be Free." *Silk & Soul.* Written by Billy Taylor, produced by Danny Davis. RCA Records, released in 1967.

————. "It's Nobody's Fault but Mine." *Nina Simone and Piano!* Written by Nina Simone, produced by Stroud Productions. RCA Studios, released in 1969.

————. "Mississippi Goddam." *Nina Simone in Concert.* Written by Nina Simone, produced by Hal Mooney. Philips Records, released in 1964.

————. "My Baby Just Cares for Me." *Little Girl Blue.* Written by Walter Donaldson and Gus Kahn. Bethlehem Records, released in February 1959.

————. "Stars." [Live at the 1976 Montreux Jazz Festival] Written by Janis Ian. https://www.youtube.com/watch?v=zsa2Aohq3-0.

————. "To Be Young, Gifted and Black." *Black Gold.* Written by Nina Simone and Weldon Irvine, produced by Stroud Productions. RCA Victor, released in 1970.

Index